# Practicing Management

# Practicing Management

Alan S. Gutterman

**BEP** BUSINESS EXPERT PRESS

*Practicing Management*

First published in 2019 by
Business Expert Press, LLC
222 East 46th Street, New York, NY 10017
www.businessexpertpress.com

ISBN-13: 978-1-94999-123-9 (paperback)
ISBN-13: 978-1-94999-124-6 (e-book)

Business Expert Press Human Resource Management and Organizational Behavior Collection

Collection ISSN: 1946-5637 (print)
Collection ISSN: 1946-5645 (electronic)

Cover and interior design by Exeter Premedia Services Private Ltd., Chennai, India

First edition: 2019

10 9 8 7 6 5 4 3 2 1

Printed in the United States of America.

# Abstract

A wide range of definitions and conceptualizations of "management" have been offered and it is often difficult for managers to fully and clearly understand their roles within the organization; however, managers striving for effectiveness and success would do well to invest time and effort into understanding the functions, roles, and skills associated with the managerial position. As with definitions of management, researchers and commentators have developed a variety of lists of managerial functions. The consensus seems to be that managers can expect to be involved in planning, organizing, leading, and controlling, and that these functions will be needed when working with a range of organizational resources including people, cash, physical assets, and information. While the specific day-to-day activities of managers will vary depending on his or her place in the organizational hierarchy, he or she must nonetheless have the ability to understand the behaviors and feelings of the people who report to them, senior officials above them in the organizational hierarchy, other colleagues throughout the organization, and external stakeholders such as customers, suppliers, and regulators. In addition, managers must be able to maintain self-awareness and monitor their personal capacities for dealing with the stress of their jobs and engaging in activities that will further their career development. In order to be adroit practitioners of their craft, managers must understand certain basic concepts such as the functions, roles, and skills associated with the managerial position; the different levels of managerial effectiveness and how they are measured; and the styles available to managers, and the factors that determine which style might be preferred in a particular instance. This book addresses a wide array of topics relating to the practice of management including the roles and activities expected from an effective manager; specific skills which can be learned and perfected by persons that aspire to management positions; styles of management; management systems; and managing in developing countries.

# Keywords

management; managerial roles and activities; management skills; management styles; management systems; organizational performance; managing in developing countries

# Contents

Chapter 1    Management Roles and Activities ....................................1

Chapter 2    Management Skills ........................................39

Chapter 3    Management Styles........................................71

Chapter 4    Management Systems ....................................89

Chapter 5    Managing in Developing Countries............................119

*About the Author*............................................................165

*Index* ........................................................................167

# CHAPTER 1

# Management Roles and Activities

## Introduction

In order to understand whether someone is being an effective manager it is necessary to have some idea of the expectations regarding the person's roles and activities within the organization. A number of different approaches have been taken in creating models of managerial functions or activities. Fayol famously argued that there were five principle managerial functions—planning, organizing, commanding, coordinating, and controlling—and others have accepted these categories and added a handful of others such as staffing and rewarding. Mintzberg criticized Fayol's "five functions" as being an inaccurate reflection of the complex and chaotic nature of the manager's tasks and suggested an alternative model of the ten core "roles," or organized sets of behaviors, identified with a managerial position, which he divided up into three groups: interpersonal roles, informational roles, and decisional roles. Others have pointed out that it is useful to distinguish between "functional" and "general" managers, each of whom have their own unique duties, responsibilities, and skill requirements. Finally, the position or level of the manager in the organizational hierarchy is likely to be relevant to his or her roles and activities: "first-line" managers focus primarily on supervision of operational employees, "middle managers" focus primarily on supervising the first-line managers and/or staff departments, and "top-level" or "senior" managers focus on setting the strategic direction for the entire organization.[1]

---

[1] Managers interested in overviews of managerial roles, activities, skills and styles should review Belker, L.B., J. McCormick, and G.S. Topchik. 2012. *The First Time Manager*. AMACOM Div American Mgmt Assn; Lebowitz, S. n.d. "10 Books Every First-Time Manager Should Read." https://inc.com/business-

## Models of Managerial Activities

Serious consideration of managerial roles and activities is often traced back
to the work of Henri Fayol, who was one of the first to focus on the specific
functions and roles of managers and famously observed in his writings in
the early 20th century that managers had five principle roles: planning,
organizing, commanding, coordinating, and controlling.[2] A good deal of
the management literature created since the 1950s has relied on what has
become known as the "functional approach" to management, which built
on Fayol's ideas and defined and analyzed the activities of managers and
the managerial process by reference to functions such as planning and
organizing as opposed to the traditional substantive functions such as
manufacturing, sales, and finance.[3]

Other management theorists working and writing during the 1950s
and 1960s also embraced what became known as the "process school of
management," which was based on the notion that management should
be viewed as process that included an identifiable set of several interdependent functions. Like Fayol, they believed that these managerial functions
were universal and thus would be relevant and applicable to all managers
regardless of the type of organization in which they worked or their level

insider/books-new-managers-should-read.html (accessed January 29, 2016);
Blanchard, K., and S. Johnson. 2015. *The New One Minute Manager*. New York,
NY: Manjul Publishing; William, M. 2016. The Essential Manager's Handbook:
The Ultimate Visual Guide to Successful Management. London: DK Publishing;
and 2017. *The Harvard Business Review Manager's Handbook: The 17 Skills Leaders
Need to Stand Out*. Cambridge MA: Harvard Business Review Press.
[2] Fayol, H. (translated from the French edition (Dunod) by Constance Storrs),
General and Industrial Management, (Pitman: 1949). For further discussion of
these principles, see "Organizational Design: A Library of Resources for Sustainable Entrepreneurs" prepared and distributed by the Sustainable Entrepreneurship Project (www.seproject.org).
[3] Adapted from Barnett, T. n.d. "Encyclopedia of Management: Management
Functions." https://referenceforbusiness.com/management/Log-Mar/Manage-
ment-Functions.html (accessed December 14, 2018).

within a particular organizational structure.[4] For example, Koontz et al. identified the following five activities as "major management functions"[5]:

- Planning: Predetermining a course of action for accomplishing organizational objectives
- Organizing: Arranging the relationships among work units for accomplishment of objectives and the granting of responsibility and authority to obtain those objectives
- Staffing: Selecting and training people for positions in the organization
- Directing: Creating an atmosphere that will assist and motivate people to achieve desired end results (sometimes referred to as "leading")
- Controlling: Establishing, measuring, and evaluating performance of activities toward planned objectives

The process school of management, and the accompanying functions described earlier, remained the dominant analytical framework into the early 1970s when critics began to argue that Fayol's "five functions" were too "normative and functional" and failed to adequately capture the complexity of a manager's daily activities and the significant amount of time that managers must devote to nurturing informal relationships with subordinates and other parties outside of the organization in order to motivate the workforce, communicate their goals and ideas, and collect information about the organization's external environment that can be used for planning.[6] Perhaps the strongest opposition came from Mintzberg, who argued that the process school of management and its emphasis on tightly defined functional categories did not accurately reflect the complex and chaotic nature of the manager's tasks. Mintzberg

---

[4] See, e.g., Koontz, H., and C. O'Donnell. 1955. *Principles of Management: An Analysis of Managerial Functions.* New York, NY: McGraw-Hill Book Co.

[5] Koontz, H., C. O'Donnell, and H. Weihrich. 1970. *Management,* 7th ed. New York, NY: McGraw-Hill.

[6] Henri Fayol. n.d. "Five Functions of Management." http://provenmodels.com/3 (accessed December 15, 2018).

suggested an alternative model of "managerial roles" and generated a fair amount of debate regarding the validity of the process school of management. Several empirical studies were conducted to determine whether Fayol or Mintzberg had the most "accurate" model for managerial activities and the conclusion seemed to be that both approaches were useful and valid ways to describe and analyze the work of managers.[7]

In recent years other suggestions and descriptions of managerial roles and duties have been put forth by scholars and consultants working in a number of different disciplines. For example, Noe, writing about the relationship between strategy and training, argued that managers have a number of key roles and duties at companies that use high-performance work practices[8]:

- Managing Alignment: Clarifying team and company goals; helping employees manage their objectives and scanning the organizational environment for useful information for the team
- Coordinating Activities: Ensuring that the team is meeting internal and external customer needs; ensuring that the team meets it quantity and quality objectives; helping the team resolve problems with other teams and ensuring uniformity in the interpretation of policies and procedures
- Facilitating Decision-Making Processes: Facilitating team decision-making and helping the team use effective decision-making processes (i.e., dealing with conflicts and statistical process controls)
- Encouraging Continuous Learning: Helping the team identify training needs; helping the team become effective at "on the job" training and creating an environment that encourages learning

---

[7] See, e.g., Carroll, S., and D. Gillen. 1980. "Are the Classical Management Functions Useful in Describing Managerial Work?" *Academy of Management Review* 12, no. 1, pp. 38–51; and Lamond, D. 2004. "A Matter of Style: Reconciling Henri and Henry." *Management Decision* 42, no. 2, pp. 330–56.

[8] Noe, R. 2016. *Employee Training and Development*, 6th ed. New York, NY: McGraw-Hill Higher Education.

- Creating and Maintaining Trust: Ensuring that each team member is responsible for his or her work load and customers; treating all team members with respect and listening and responding honestly to team ideas

## Fayol's Primary Functions of Management

Henri Fayol pioneered the notion of "functions of management" in his 1916 book "Administration Industrielle et Generale" in which he identified and described five functions of managers—planning, organizing, commanding, coordinating, and controlling—that he believed were universal and required of all managers as they went about performing their day-to-day activities regardless of whether they were operating in the business environment or overseeing the activities of governmental, military, religious, or philanthropic organizations.[9] Fayol also prescribed 14 general principles of management and organization that were intended to provide managers with further guidance on how they might effectively execute their five primary management functions. At the time, Fayol was the managing director of a large coal mining firm in France and most of his ideas were based in large part on his own experiences as a manager as opposed to classical empirical research.

Fayol's work was not widely known outside of France until 1949 when his book was first published in English.[10] Nonetheless, his ideas had already begun to appear in the emerging area of management studies. For example, in 1937 Gulick and Urwick coined the acronym "POSDCORB" to refer to their own collection of seven management activities that included the five suggested by Fayol as well as two additional items: reporting and budgeting. These activities have been described as follows[11]:

---

[9] While descriptions of Fayol's model generally include the five functions mentioned in the text, some interpretations substitute the term "monitoring" for "controlling" and add "forecasting" as another distinguishable managerial function.

[10] Fayol, H. 1949. *General and Industrial Administration*. London: Sir Issac Pitman & Sons, Ltd.

[11] Gulick, L., and L. Urwick. "Description Derived from Unit 8 Classical Approach." https://scribd.com/doc/219782116/Public-Administration-Unit-8-

- Planning (P): working out the things that need to be done and the methods for doing them to accomplish the purpose set for the enterprise
- Organizing (O): establishment of the formal structure of authority through which work sub-divisions are arranged, defined, and coordinated for the defined objective
- Staffing (S): the whole personnel function of bringing in and training the staff and maintaining favorable conditions of work
- Directing (D): continuous task of making decisions and embodying them in specific and general orders and instructions, and serving as the leader of the enterprise
- Coordinating (CO): The all-important duty of inter-relating the various parts of the work
- Reporting (R): keeping the executive informed as to what is going on, which thus includes keeping himself and his subordinates informed through records, research, and inspection
- Budgeting (B): all that goes with budgeting in the form of fiscal planning, accounting, and control

## Mackenzie's 3-D Model of the Management Process

While there was little that was new in Mackenzie's "three dimensional" model of the management process presented in the late 1960s, it did provide an interesting alternative way of looking at the activities, functions, and basic elements of the manager's job.[12] Mackenzie began with an observation that managers must deal with three basic elements as they go about their day-to-day activities—ideas, things, and people—and noted

---

Classical-Approach-Luther-Gulick-and-Lyndall-Urwick (accessed December 15, 2018). The model proposed by Gulick and Urwick first appeared in Gulick, L., and L. Urwick., eds. 1937. *Papers on the Science of Administration*. New York, NY: Institute of Public Administration.

[12] The discussion in the section of Mackenzie's model is adapted from Mackenzie, R. November/December 1969. "The Management Process in 3-D." *Harvard Business Review*, pp. 80–87.

that these elements aligned themselves with three essential skill sets: conceptual thinking, particularly planning, administration, and leadership. He pointed out that organizations needed managers who were adroit at practicing each of these skill sets (i.e., planners, administrators, and leaders); however, he conceded that someone who was good at one set of skills may not be good at the others. Common illustrations included situations where someone might be a strong charismatic leader who could easily motivate people yet be weak in areas such as planning and management that required conceptual skills.

Mackenzie then went to suggest two categories of managerial functions: "sequential" and "continuous." The list and description of the sequential functions applied to each specific work activity or undertaking, such as development and launch of a new product. The following five sequential functions were identified as proceeding in the following order:

- Planning, described as "predetermining" a course of action. Specific planning activities included development of policies and procedures, budgeting and programming, development of strategies and setting objectives, and forecasting.
- Organizing, described as arranging and relating work and specific jobs in a manner that allowed for effective accomplishment of objectives. Specific organizing activities included establishing job qualifications and descriptions and establishing the organizational structure and delineating relationships within that structure.
- Staffing, described as selecting competent people for each of the positions established within the organizational structure during the organizing phase. Staffing activities included recruitment and selection, orientation, training, and development.
- Directing, described as bringing about purposeful action toward the desired goals and objectives. The direction phase required delegation, motivation, coordination, conflict resolution, and change management.
- Control, described as ensuring progress toward the objectives that were established during the planning phase. Control

activities included establishing reporting systems, developing performance standards, measuring results, establishing reward systems, and taking corrective actions.

Mackenzie also included definitions and descriptions of each of the actions that he associated with the various functions. For example, with respect to planning, the "forecasting" activity was defined as making sure to "establish where present course of action will lead" and the "budgeting" activity was the steps taken to "allocate resources." With respect to directing, the "coordination" activity included making sure to "relate efforts in most effective combination" and the "change management" activity focused on strategies to "stimulate creativity and innovation in achieving goals." Mackenzie suggested that managers pay particular attention to each of these supplemental definitions and descriptions when they were focusing their time and interest on one specific sequential function.

Each of the three skill sets mentioned earlier played an important role in the flow of sequential functions. For example, ideas and conceptual thinking were the cornerstones of planning, things and administration were at the forefront of organizing, and the last three of the sequential functions—staffing, directing, and controlling—all turned on influencing and effectively leading people within the organization. Mackenzie noted that the sequential process continuously repeated itself as feedback collected and analyzed during the control phase was used to make adjustments to the plan which then triggered changes all the way along the cycle (e.g., modifications to the organizational structure, recruitment of new employees with different qualifications and/or changes in the performance standards and reward systems).

The "continuous," or "general," functions in Mackenzie's model occurred throughout the management process rather than in a particular sequence and included analyzing problems, making decisions, and communicating. Mackenzie explained that decisions must be made, and problems identified and resolved, during each of the planning, organizing, directing, and controlling phases and that communication was also continuously needed to ensure that directions were disseminated and plans were explained to, and understood by, everyone in the organization. Once again, there were obvious and strong links between these continuous functions and the three skill sets mentioned earlier. For example, conceptual thinking was needed in order to analyze problems and communication skills were needed in order to motivate and lead people within the organization.

## Bloom and Van Reenen's Management Practices

As part of their exhaustive study of international patterns of management and productivity in 17 countries, Bloom and Van Reenen identified 18 basic management practices or dimensions that were placed into the following three broad areas for purposes of comparison: "monitoring management," which focused on how well managers monitored what was going on inside their firms and used this information for continuous improvement; "targets management," which focused on whether or not managers set the right targets for their firms, tracked the right outcomes for their firms, and then took appropriate action when the targets and outcomes were inconsistent; and "incentives management," which focused on whether managers promoted and rewarded employees based on performance and tried to hire and keep their best employees.[13]

Evaluation and assessment of each of the three types of management was based on average across five to seven questions for each type and these questions could be used by managers to identify activities and

---

[13] Bloom, N., and J. Van Reenen. Winter 2010. "Why Do Management Practices Differ across Firms and Countries." *Journal of Economic Perspectives* 24, no. 1, pp. 203–24, 206. Bloom and Van Reenen noted that the chosen areas were similar to those emphasized by other researchers such as Ichinowski, C., K. Shaw, and G. Prenushi. 1997. "The Effects of Human Resource Management: A Study of Steel Finishing Lines." *American Economic Review*, pp. 291–313; Black, S., and L. Lynch. 2001. "How to Compete: The Impact of Workplace Practices and Information Technology on Productivity." *Review of Economics and Statistics* 83, no. 3, pp. 434–45. They also noted the work of Bertrand and Schoar that focused on the management styles of chief executive and chief financial officers and thus provided insight into another area, "strategic management," which is particular relevant for managers at the top of the organizational hierarchy. See Bertrand, M., and A. Schoar. 2003. "Managing with Style: The Effect of Managers on Firm Policies." *Quarterly Journal of Economics*, pp. 1169–208.

projects that Bloom and Van Reenen considered to be significant. For example, scores with respect to "incentives management" were based on a set of questions that focused on whether managers promoted and rewarded employees based on performance and trying to hire and keep their best employees. Specific topics included managing human capital, rewarding high performance, removing poor performers, promoting high performers, and attracting and retaining human capital. Scores with respect to "monitoring management" were based on a set of questions that focused on how well managers monitor what goes on inside their firms and use this information for continuous improvement. Specific topics included introduction of modern manufacturing techniques and the rationale for introducing such techniques, process problem documentation, performance tracking and review and performance dialogue. Finally, scores with respect to "targets management" were based on a set of questions that focused on whether or not managers set the right targets for their firms, track the right outcomes for their firms, and then take appropriate action when targets and outcomes are inconsistent. Specific topics included target balance and interconnection, target time horizon, whether the targets are stretching and performance clarity.[14]

## Mintzberg's "Management Roles"

Mintzberg's classic mid-1970s article on "The Manager's Job" focused on the basic question of "what do managers do?" and argued that without a proper answer to this question it was difficult, if not impossible, to teach and train managers, improve the practice of management, and design planning or information systems for managers that would be useful to

---

[14] A full set of questions for each dimension appears in Bloom, N., and J. Van Reenen. 2006. "Measuring and Explaining Management Practices Across Firms and Countries." *Centre for Economic Performance Discussion Paper*, p. 716. See also "Comparative Management Studies" prepared and distributed by the Sustainable Entrepreneurship Project (www.seproject.org) and Bloom, N., and J. Van Reenen. n.d. "New Approaches to Surveying Organizations." http://stanford.edu/~bloom/Surveying_AER.pdf

them in their day-to-day activities.[15] Mintzberg noted that the common shorthand description of the activities of managers had long been based on the ideas first suggested by Fayol: planning, organization, coordination, and control. However, Mintzberg's extensive surveys of the characteristics and content of other research on managerial work, as well as his own studies and observations, led him to challenge several "myths" about managerial work that he believed were not credible "under careful scrutiny of the facts." Among other things, Mintzberg reviewed topics such as how long managers worked and where, at what pace managers worked and what types of interruptions occurred in their activities, through what media did managers communicate, and what activities did managers actually carry out and why.[16] Based on all of this he proposed his own descriptive model of the ten core "roles," or organized sets of behaviors, identified with a managerial position, which he divided up into three groups: interpersonal roles, informational roles, and decisional roles. While Mintzberg described the ten core managerial roles separately, he conceded that "these ten roles are not easily separable ... [n]o role can be pulled out of the framework and the job be left intact." He did find, however, that managers varied in terms of how much emphasis they placed on particular activities and that variations often could be traced to a manager's primary functional focus: sales managers spent more time on interpersonal roles, a finding that Mintzberg noted might be related to the "extrovert nature" of sales and marketing activities; production managers focused on decisional roles, which would appear to make sense given their responsibilities with respect to ensuring that work flows efficiently within the organizations; and staff managers were more attentive to informational roles, which should not be surprising given that there primary value to the organization is providing "expert advice" to various departments.

---

[15] Mintzberg, H. July–August 1975. "The Manager's Job: Folklore and Fact." *Harvard Business Review* 53, no. 4, pp. 49–61. In general, material presented as a quotation in the discussion of Mintzberg's model in this section and the follow sections is excerpted from the Mintzberg article.

[16] Information regarding Mintzberg's own studies of managerial work was collected in Mintzberg, H. 1973. *The Nature of Managerial Work.* New York, NY: Harper & Row.

## Folklore and Facts about Managerial Roles and Activities

The first bit of "folklore" regarding a manager noted by Mintzberg was that he or she is a "reflective, systematic planner." However, Mintzberg argued that the actual evidence on this issue, which he described as "overwhelming," was "that managers work at a unrelenting pace, that their activities are characterized by brevity, variety, and discontinuity, and that they are strongly oriented to action and dislike reflective activities." Based on a variety of sources, including diary studies and surveys of the verbal contacts of chief executive officers, Mintzberg concluded that most of the planning done by managers was done "implicitly in the context of daily actions," rather than as part of some abstract process in a retreat setting, and that the plans that managers did have "seemed to exist only in their heads—as flexible, but often specific, intentions."

The second "myth" of managerial activities addressed by Mintzberg was the notion that the effective manager had no regular duties to perform and should take advantage of his position to delegate actions to others in the organization so that he or she can spend time planning and being available to deal with unforeseen events that require his or her input. Mintzberg referred to the popular analogy of a "good manager" to a "good conductor" who "carefully orchestrates everything in advance, then sits back, responding occasionally to an unforeseeable exception." Under this model of a manager, he or she is removed from activities such as meeting with customers or leading negotiations. However, Mintzberg's analysis of the evidence on "managerial duties" led to a very different conclusion, specifically that "managerial work involves performing a number of regular duties, including ritual and ceremony, negotiations, and processing of soft information that links the organization with its environment."

The need and ability of effective managers to tap into soft external information that only he or she could access due to his or her position and then process and disseminate that information throughout the organization was related to Mintzberg's criticisms of a third bit of "folklore," namely the idea that senior managers needed "aggregated information" that is best provided through a formal management information system ("MIS"). Mintzberg noted that the design of complex information systems had become one of the most popular themes of management studies over the decades prior to the release of his article; however, Mintzberg observed that the tremendous investment of time, capital, and human resources in MIS has perhaps been misplaced in light of evidence that managers were not using these systems and instead relied primarily on "verbal media, telephone calls and meetings" rather than documents and reports generated by those systems. In addition, Mintzberg suggested that the evidence indicates that managers preferred "specific tidbits of data" rather than "hard" information generated by MIS to carry out two important activities that required information: identification of problems and opportunities and development of mental models regarding core issues and activities such as budgeting and the customer's process of deciding how to select and purchase products.

Finally, Mintzberg took issue with the whole idea that management was on its way to becoming both a science and a profession. Mintzberg argued that neither of these conclusions could be true unless and until one was able to know what procedures managers use, a precondition to the systemic analysis associated with "science," and what managers are supposed to learn so that it was possible to identify when a manager has achieved the requisite level of learning to qualify as a professional in the field.[17] Instead, according to Mintzberg, the specifics of the "programming" conducted by managers—scheduling their time, obtaining and processing information, and making decisions—remained locked in their minds and occurred in a complex process that was difficult to explain, predict, model, and teach to others. Mintzberg noted that the very "unscientific" concepts of "judgment" and "intuition" were very much a part of what drove managers to do what they do.

## Interpersonal Roles

Mintzberg explained that three of the managerial roles that he had identified "arise directly from formal authority and involve basic interpersonal relationships." These interpersonal roles involved interactions and

---

[17] Mintzberg cited the definition of "profession" in the Random House Dictionary as involving "knowledge of some department of learning or science."

relationships with persons within the organization and with persons representing outside constituencies. The first of these roles was that of a "figurehead" and focused on the various ceremonial duties that managers were expected to perform in their position as the head of a unit of the organization. Mintzberg noted that while some of these activities, such as greeting visitors touring the facility or taking a customer out to lunch, may be "routine" and do not involve serious business communications they were nonetheless important for the organization to function smoothly. The second role was that of "leader" and Mintzberg commented that "the influence of managers is most clearly seen in the leader role."[18] Leadership could be both direct, as when the manager makes decisions about who to hire for his or her staff and how they are used and trained, and indirect, as when managers set the overall goals for the organization and engage in behaviors calculated to motivate and encourage employees that the managers may not see on a day-to-day basis. Mintzberg observed that leadership is the major determinant of how effective a manager would be in exercising the substantial amount of formal power that is vested in him or her by virtue of his or her position. Finally, the last interpersonal role was that of "liaison" and included the time that managers spent on "contacts outside the vertical chain of command." Mintzberg reported that "managers spend as much time with peers and other people outside their units as they do with their own subordinates—and, surprisingly, very little time with their own superiors." Specifically, Mintzberg noted that the respondents in his own study—CEOs of various organizations—averaged 44 percent of their contact time with people outside their organizations, 48 percent with subordinates, and 7 percent with directors and trustees, and that the "outsiders" included clients, business associates, suppliers, managers of similar organizations, government and trade organization

---

[18] Mintzberg is not the only one to include "leadership" among the key managerial functions. See, e.g., Jones, G., J. George, and C. Hill. 2000. *Contemporary Management*, 2nd ed. New York, NY: Irwin/McGraw-Hill (management is "the process of using an organization's resources to achieve specific goals through the functions of planning, organizing, leading and controlling"). Inclusion of "leadership" in conceptualizations of management is often justified by explaining that leadership is an important element of the directing function of management.

officials, and fellow directors on outside boards.[19] Mintzberg cautioned that mastery and effectiveness of the various interpersonal roles would take time and patience and that, for example, it would be foolish to assume that a new manager would have the same broad liaison network as a manager who had been on the job for a number of years and thus had the time to develop the necessary relationships.

## Informational Roles

The interpersonal roles described earlier, which involved a substantial amount of contact with persons inside and outside the organization, provided the manager with a substantial amount of information that is relevant to the operation and progress of the organizational unit and Mintzberg identified three additional roles that were based on the manager's activities in processing and communicating information. First of all, a manager was expected to serve as a "monitor" who continuously scanned the environment for information that he or she could extract from subordinates, his or her external network, and from unsolicited sources. Second, since the manager sat at the top and in the middle of the organizational hierarchy created by him or her in the "leader" role he or she could act as the "disseminator" who communicated information to subordinates who might not otherwise have access to such information and needed it in order to perform their jobs. The disseminator role also included passing information from one subordinate to another in situations where the two subordinates might not otherwise have direct contact, an activity which facilitates coordination within the organization. Mintzberg mentioned that the disseminator role could be used to illustrate how all of the roles in his model were tightly integrated and often impossible to separate. Specifically, he pointed out that unless a manager recognizes his or her liaison role and seeks and obtains information from external sources, he or she will be unable to provide the necessary support in the disseminator role

---

[19] Mintzberg, H. July–August 1975. "The Manager's Job: Folklore and Fact." *Harvard Business Review* 53, no. 4, pp. 49–61 (referring to studies summarized in Mintzberg, H. 1973. *The Nature of Managerial Work*. New York, NY: Harper & Row).

since he or she does not have information that should be disseminated to employees to support their efforts to perform in a manner that addresses the external conditions confronting the organization. In other words, mastery of the disseminator role requires not only communications skills but also an ability and willingness to collect and analyze the most relevant information from liaison contacts. Finally, information was the basis for the communications that a manager made as the chief "spokesperson" for his or her organizational unit. For example, the manager might represent his or her organizational unit by communicating with directors and shareholders, consumer groups, government officials and suppliers, and other business partners. The spokesperson role also included certain communications to influential persons within the organization, such as when the manager passed information about decisions on the volume and flow of work to group leaders who were responsible for coordinating the activities of the subordinates under their control.

## Decisional Roles

Mintzberg noted that by virtue of his or her formal position at the top of the hierarchy for the organizational unit and the focal point for collection and processing of information "the manager plays the major role in the unit's decision-making system." The manager's position meant that only he or she could make certain decisions that set the direction for the organization's activities and the manager's access to information meant that he or she was uniquely situated to make the most informed decisions regarding key issues such as the overall organizational strategy, new initiatives, and allocation of resources. Mintzberg described the following four roles of a manager as a "decision maker:"

- As the "entrepreneur" the manager selected, initiated, and oversaw activities that would hopefully improve the organizational unit and allow it to adapt to, and successfully compete in, a continuously changing external environment. Mintzberg referred to those activities as "development projects" and noted that the CEOs he had surveyed survey juggled as many as 50 of them at any one time as they moved through various stages of maturation and continuously changed the inventory of projects they were working on to emphasize some, discard others, and bring new ones online. Mintzberg provided a descriptive list of common development projects, including new products or processes, public relations campaigns, improvement of cash position, organizational restructure to bolster weaknesses in particular areas, resolution of morale problems, integration of computer operations, and acquisitions.

- While entrepreneurship involved voluntary attempts to initiate change, the manager's role as the "disturbance handler" focused on involuntary responses to events and pressures for change that were outside of the manager's reasonable control (e.g., a major customer runs into financial difficulties or a supplier breaches its commitment to provide materials). While good managers always engaged in some form of contingency planning to anticipate risks and environmental disturbances, no such planning system was perfect and inevitably a fair amount of managerial time must be spent on "putting out fires." As for bad managers, they generally ignored, or didn't even see, potential problems until they reached a crisis point.

- As the "resource allocator," the manager made decisions about "who will get what," starting with the manager's own time and attention and then continuing on to the wide array of choices that must be made regarding division and coordination of work and investment of capital and human resources. Interestingly, Mintzberg claimed that the CEOs he studied often made authorization decisions on an "ad hoc basis" rather than relying heavily on complex and expensive capital budgeting systems and procedures and that managers were prone to approving specific projects based on the people involved rather than a deep analysis of the particular proposal.

- The role of "negotiator" was an important activity for all managers given that they were the ones with the final authority to commit the resources of the organization, determine the workflow within the organization, and choose between

competing projects and interests. Managers were also particularly suited to participating in negotiating activities, such as
hammering out the terms of a contract with a key supplier or
resolving interdepartmental disputes, because of the treasure
trove of information they collected as they carried out their
other roles and responsibilities.

## Functional versus General Managers

It is often argued that there are real and important differences between
managers that have "functional" duties and responsibilities and those
that have "general management" duties and responsibilities. As the category names imply, functional managers focus on activities in a single
functional area while general managers have broader responsibilities overseeing the entire organization or a business unit that includes
functional-based departments. The size of the organization appears to
be a significant factor in the creation and proliferation of functional
management positions, with growth in size leading to more and more
managerial specialization in areas such as marketing and finance. In contrast, smaller organizations rely more heavily on general managers who
are actively involved in all operational areas of the business. It is possible
for functional managers to transition to general management and organizations are well advised to provide managers making such a transition
with adequate training, particularly since new general managers must
learn how to see the connections and linkages within the entire organizational structure and wean themselves off of the comfort zone provided
by their functional expertise.

## Responsibilities of Functional Managers

Functional managers are responsible for the activities of departments and
other work groups formed and organized to concentrate on functional
activities such as accounting, research and development, manufacturing,
sales and marketing. In most instances, functional managers have education, training, experience, and technical skills that make them "functional
experts" and functional groups tend to be relatively homogenous with

members have similar backgrounds and training and focused on performing tasks that are similar and closely related. Functional managers are often promoted from within the ranks of their departments or work groups, typically after progressing through several jobs and levels within the department or group. Functional managers must not only stay abreast of developments in their area but must also develop an understanding of how their department or group is expected to interact with other work units in the organization. It is also incumbent on the functional manager to be able to provide information to members of his or her department or group and educate them about how their activities fit into the overall operations of the organization.[20] As noted earlier, Mintzberg suggested that variations among managers with respect to their emphasis on particular managerial activities and core managerial roles could be traced to a manager's primary functional focus and thus it would not be surprising to find sales and marketing managers investing more time and effort in interpersonal roles while production managers were more likely to be focusing on decisional roles.[21]

## Responsibilities of General Managers

While functional managers are primarily concerned with a single function, the duties and responsibilities of general managers include making sure that several functional groups or other parts of the organizational structure work together effectively.[22] The main job of a general manager is not to match the technical skills and expertise of the managers of the functional groups that they oversee but rather to make sure that the activities of those groups are coordinated and integrated to the degree necessary to achieve the goals and objectives of the organization as a whole. The duties and responsibilities of a particular general manager depend on the business activities of his or her organization. For example,

---

[20] Lewis, P., S. Goodman, P. Fandt, and J. Michlitsch. 2007. *Management: Challenges for Tomorrow's Leaders*, 9, 5th ed. Mason, OH: Thomson South-Western.

[21] Mintzberg, H. July–August 1975. "The Manager's Job: Folklore and Fact." *Harvard Business Review* 53, no. 4, pp. 49–61.

[22] Id.

when the organizational structure is based on the functions necessary to develop and commercialize a specific product the general manager will be coordinating groups focused on research and development, procurement, manufacturing, sales, marketing, and customer service. On the other hand, the general, or branch, manager of a supermarket may need to coordinate groups organized by different types of products dispersed around the store, such as produce, groceries, bakery goods, meat and poultry, and flowers.[23]

## Levels of Management

Another way to assess managerial activities and skill requirements is to focus on "levels of management." The general view is that there are three levels of managers in the organizational hierarchy of companies that have survived the start-up stage and grown to the point where their portfolio of operations is relatively mature. These levels are commonly referred to as "first-line" managers, who focus primarily on supervision of operational employees; "middle managers," who focus primarily on supervising the first-line managers and/or staff departments; and, finally, "top-level," or "senior," managers, who should be focusing on setting the strategic direction for the entire organization. Larger organizations generally have more first-line managers than middle managers and more middle managers than senior managers, a situation that is depicted in the traditional triangular structure of the organizational hierarchy that puts operational personnel at the bottom and then layers first-line, middle, and senior managers above them.[24]

Numerous studies have been conducted regarding the activities and required skills of the three levels of managers. It is generally conceded that all managers, regardless of their specific titles, roles, and placement in the organizational hierarchy, will be called upon to engage in planning, organizing, leading, and controlling at some point; however, the amount of time and effort spent on these activities by managers varies significantly depending on which level they are on in the organizational

---

[23] Id.

[24] Id.

hierarchy. For example, Weihrich observed: "All managers carry out the functions of planning, organizing, staffing, leading, and controlling, although the time spent in each function will differ and the skills required by managers at different organizational levels vary.... The managerial activities, grouped into the managerial functions of planning, organizing, staffing, leading, and controlling, are carried out by all managers, but the practices and methods must be adapted to the particular tasks, enterprises and situation."[25] He noted that this concept was sometimes referred to as the "universality of management" because the functions performed by managers remained constant regardless of their place in the organizational hierarchy or the type of activities engaged in by the organization. Variability in the activities of managers at different levels also translates into differences in the specific skills that managers need to have and rely upon in carrying out their immediate duties and responsibilities. Thus, for example, technical skills tend to be more important for first-line managers, although they do employ human and conceptual skills during their activities, human skills are the most important for middle managers, and conceptual skills are the most relevant for senior managers.[26]

## First-Line Managers

First-line managers can be thought of as those persons that are responsible for supervising the activities of operational employees who are directly responsible for production of the company's products or delivery of the company's services.[27] A broad range of titles are bestowed on these

---

[25] See Weihrich, H. 2004. "Management: Science, Theory, and Practice." In *Essentials of Management: An International Perspective*, eds. Weihrich and Koontz. https://scribd.com/document/106629608/22550642-Management-Science-Theory-and-Practice (accessed December 14, 2018).

[26] Lewis, P., S. Goodman, P. Fandt, and J. Michlitsch. 2007. *Management: Challenges for Tomorrow's Leaders*, 9, 5th ed. Mason, OH: Thomson South-Western.

[27] The discussion of the activities and skills of first-line managers in this section is adapted from Lewis, P., S. Goodman, P. Fandt, and J. Michlitsch. 2007. *Management: Challenges for Tomorrow's Leaders*, 9–10, 5th ed. Mason, OH: Thomson South-Western.

first-line managers, including "production supervisor," "line manager," "section chief," or "account manager." While they are relatively low in the overall organizational hierarchy, the responsibilities of first-line managers are absolutely crucial to the success of the company: making sure that the products and services of the company are delivered to customers on time on a daily basis at the expected quality levels. First-line managers are typically promoted from within the ranks based on their mastery of the relevant technical skills and their ability to manage others with respect to attaining, using, and improving those technical skills. Accordingly, technical skills are generally considered to be the most important of the three general skills described earlier for first-line managers.

First-line managers also need to have strong human skills in order to instruct subordinates on the required technical skills and manage the individual performance of those subordinates. As an instructor, a first-line manager needs to be adept at training, coaching, and instructing, activities that require an ability to communicate as well as a deep knowledge of the relevant technical tools, techniques, and procedures. As a performance manager, a first-line manager must be able to motivate subordinates, monitor the performance of subordinates and provide feedback, discipline subordinates when necessary and, finally, continuously improve communications with subordinates in order to train and coach them and make sure that products and services are delivered in the manner required by the organization's strategic plan.

While the day-to-day activities of first-line managers generally do not call for the same amount of conceptual or design skills required of managers higher in the organizational hierarchy, first-line managers are nonetheless charged with various planning and scheduling responsibilities that are related to meeting deadlines for delivery of products and services. In companies where senior management has delegated a lot of authority downward and declined to rely heavily on formal rules and procedures, first-line managers have a good deal of autonomy with respect to organizing and controlling the subordinates that they manage. On the other hand, if control and decision-making responsibilities are centralized and senior management has promulgated detailed written rules and procedures, the latitude of first-line managers is severely restricted and opportunities to use conceptual skills are limited.

# Middle Managers

Middle managers are responsible for overseeing and supervising the activities of first-level managers or staff departments.[28] Commonly used titles for middle managers include "department head," product manager" or "marketing manager." As a general rule, middle managers are elevated from the ranks of first-line managers in the particular area or department in which they specialize; however, middle managers are sometimes brought in from other areas of the organizational structure in cases where technical skills are not overly important in effectively doing the job and the candidate has demonstrated that he or she has the necessary human skills and grasp of overall organizational strategy and the steps that need to be taken in order to effectively implement that strategy.

From their place in the "middle" of the organizational hierarchy, it is apparent that middle managers must be effective in establishing linkages between the first-line managers that they oversee and senior management, including making sure that first-line managers understand the organizational strategy and how they fit into it and also facilitating the flow of feedback from lower levels of the organizational hierarchy up to senior management so they can make appropriate and necessary changes in strategy. In addition, middle managers are relied upon to effectively allocate resources in the areas or departments they oversee and monitor the performance of first-line managers and departments to be sure that the resources are being used in a manner that promotes achievement of organizational goals.

Lewis et al. observed that there are three basic activities for which middle managers are responsible: planning and allocation of resources, coordination of interdependent groups, and management of group performance. The various coordination and group management activities explain why it is so important for middle managers to have good "human skills." For example, those types of skills are needed to coordinate the

---

[28] The discussion of the activities and skills of middle managers in this section is adapted from Lewis, P., S. Goodman, P. Fandt, and J. Michlitsch. 2007. *Management: Challenges for Tomorrow's Leaders*, 10–11, 5th ed. Mason, OH: Thomson South-Western.

activities of members of the work group that the middle manager oversees. In addition, human skills are essential to being an effective liaison with other work groups in different parts of the organizational structure, specifically working to obtain resources from other departments, resolve conflicts with those departments, and gather information from those departments that can be shared with members of the middle manager's work group. Finally, motivating and inspiring group members and resolving conflicts with a group both require sensitivity to the needs and concerns of the group members.

It is generally felt that human skills play the biggest role in the success or failure of a middle manager; however, technical and conceptual skills still play a role, albeit less significant than human skills, in the middle manager's day-to-day activities. For example, middle managers must have sufficient knowledge of the technical issues confronting front-line managers to understand the concerns of those managers and make constructive suggestions when front-line managers seek advice and direction. In addition, middle managers must deploy their conceptual skills when creating the operational plans for the first-level managers or staff departments that they oversee since inevitably middle managers are confronted with having to cope with scarce resources and the need to make tough decisions about how those resources are allocated.

## Top-Level or Senior Managers

Top-level, or senior, managers are primarily responsible for setting the overall strategic direction for the organization and typically have titles such as "chief executive officer," "president," "chief operating officer," "chief financial officer," and "executive vice president."[29] While the ability

---

[29] The discussion of the activities and skills of top-level, or senior, managers in this section is adapted from Lewis, P., S. Goodman, P. Fandt, and J. Michlitsch. 2007. *Management: Challenges for Tomorrow's Leaders*, 11–12, 5th ed. Mason, OH: Thomson South-Western. For further discussion of the activities and skills of the members of the executive team, see "Governance: A Library of Resources for Sustainable Entrepreneurs" prepared and distributed by the Sustainable Entrepreneurship Project (www.seproject.org).

to establish the strategic direction is the most important requirement for the chief executive officer ("CEO") and the other senior managers on the "executive team," they must also have the skills required to set a vision for the company and communicate that vision to lower-level managers and employees and lead them along the path that will ultimately result in realization of the vision. In light of these responsibilities, it is not surprising that conceptual skills are extremely important for senior managers, since those skills are needed for three important activities that can only be carried out at the top of the organizational hierarchy: collecting and processing massive amounts of information regarding both the internal and external environment of the company to identify opportunities and threats and develop an organizational strategy; evaluating the role and performance of all of the units and groups within the company and determining the best way to structure those units and groups to pursue the goals and objectives of the organization's strategy; and defining and communicating the values and norms that make up the organizational culture of the company. Design skills are also relevant to these activities since they assist senior management in identifying threats or problems in the environment and crafting strategic and structural solutions.

While senior managers can, and often do, emerge from within the company following progression from first-line management positions, the pursuit of people with requisite level of conceptual skills often leads the board of directors to look outside the company when hiring the CEO and other members of the executive team. However, successful senior managers must have more than just conceptual skills. For example, human skills are needed in order for senior managers to communicate effectively with managers and employees and work well with outside stakeholders, such as customers and other business partners (e.g., vendors and distributors), labor unions, community groups, competitors, and regulators. In addition, technical skills, particularly in areas such as finance and technologies most important to the company's business activities, are necessary in order for the senior manager to grasp the key issues associated with executing the company's strategy. Technical skills are particularly important for senior management of smaller firms since they are more closely involved with first-line activities and lack the resources to support delegation of technical details to others; however, senior managers of larger firms are generally able to rely on the technical abilities of their subordinates.[30]

## Primary Functions of Managers

While the discussion earlier illustrates that there have been a number of different approaches to defining and modeling the management process and identify specific managerial functions and activities, there is a fair amount of common ground that can be used to generate a short list of important and generally agreed "functions of managers" that would be applicable in some way to managers at all levels in the organizational structure and in each of the operating functions such as procurement, sales and marketing, and finance.[31] It is reasonable to begin such a list with Fayol's famous observation that "[t]o manage is to forecast and plan, to organize, to command, to coordinate, and to control"[32] and then perhaps add the "staffing" activity cited by both Koontz et al. and Gulick and Urwick; however, in the discussion of specific functions below staffing will be integrated into "organizing." Expanding the list much further arguably adds too much complexity and concepts such as "reporting and budgeting" might be treated as tools for coordination and control. Managers are continuously engaged in "decision-making" activities; however, this is an area that is more commonly considered in discussions of management styles that focus on the extent to which employees contribute to or participate to managerial decisions.[33] Mintzberg's behavioral

---

[30] Weihrich, H. 2004. "Management: Science, Theory, and Practice." In *Essentials of Management: An International Perspective*, eds. Weihrich and Koontz. https://scribd.com/document/106629608/22550642-Management-Science-Theory-and-Practice (accessed December 14, 2018).

[31] For discussion of how the various managerial functions described in this Guide are carried out by managers in developing countries, see "Managing in Developing Countries" prepared and distributed by the Sustainable Entrepreneurship Project (www.seproject.org).

[32] Fayol, H. 1949. *General and Industrial Administration*. London: Sir Issac Pitman & Sons, Ltd.

[33] See, e.g., Culpan, R., and O. Kucukemiroglu. 1993. "A Comparison of US and Japanese Management Styles and Unit Effectiveness." *Management International Review* 33, pp. 27–42.

approach to management activities clearly provides an interesting alternative perspective to the various functional models, but upon closer review it would appear that much of Mintzberg's model actually compliments and usefully elaborates on Fayol's ideas. For example, a manager carrying out Mintzberg's "entrepreneur" and "resource allocator" roles would be tending to engaged in the "planning" and "coordination" functions found in the Fayol model, and Mintzberg's "leadership" requires actions that fall within several of the functional categories in the Favol model including "organizing," "commanding," and "staffing."

## Planning

Planning relates to the task of creating plans of action for forecasting and coping with future conditions, including developing strategic objectives and setting attainable goals in light of the activities of the organization, the resources of the organization, and anticipated trends and developments in the organization's external environment. Simply put, "[p]lanning includes setting goals and defining the actions necessary to achieve the goals, in light of the situation."[34] Planning is perhaps the most difficult of the five functions—after all, it involves making choices about future actions from among a variety of alternatives, each of which has its own advantage, disadvantages, and risks—and requires the involvement and participation of the entire organization. While Fayol obviously believed that planning was important, he also recognized that unforeseen events would occur and thus acknowledged that plans should not be too rigid or inflexible.

Planning involves a series of steps and processes including environmental scanning, forecasts of future opportunities and threats and, finally, identification of goals and objectives for the organization and development of plans of action to achieve those goals and objectives.[35] As Fayol

---

[34] Lewis, P., S. Goodman, P. Fandt, and J. Michlitsch. 2007. *Management: Challenges for Tomorrow's Leaders*, 6, 5th ed. Mason, OH: Thomson South-Western.
[35] For further discussion of the various steps and processes associated with planning, see "Strategic Planning: A Library of Resources for Sustainable Entrepreneurs" prepared and distributed by the Sustainable Entrepreneurship Project (www.seproject.org).

noted, planners must be prepared for "contingencies" and even the best plans must be monitored to evaluate their viability and changes may be needed as new information becomes available during the planning period. Planning becomes even more challenging and complex as an organization matures and grows since plans must be developed and coordinated at different levels and with different time horizons. For example, the following distinctions have been made among strategic, tactical, and operational planning[36]:

- Strategic planning involves the classic and well-known process of so-called "SWOT analysis," including identifying the strengths ("S") and weaknesses ("W") of the organization and the competitive opportunities ("O") and threats ("T") in the external environment of the organization as a prelude to deciding how the organization should be positioned to compete and prosper. The strategic plan is the primary responsibility of the senior managers of the organization and generally has a relatively long time horizon. Involvement of senior management is essential since they are the ones best situated to define the organization's overall mission and specify goals and objectives that are tied to that mission and realistic given the results of the SWOT analysis.
- Tactical planning includes the development of specific plans of action to implement elements of the overall strategic plan. Tactical plans cover a somewhat shorter time horizon than the strategic plan—generally one to three years—and are typically assigned to mid-level managers with greater familiarity with the specific activities and resources associated with the plan.
- Operational planning has a very short time horizon, sometimes as brief as one week but typically no longer than one year, and covers very specific steps and actions that need to be completed in order to support the broader goals and

---

[36] Adapted from Barnett, T. n.d. "Encyclopedia of Management: Management Functions." https://referenceforbusiness.com/management/Log-Mar/Management-Functions.html (accessed December 14, 2018).

objectives laid out in the strategic and tactical plans. As with tactical plans, operational planning is done by managers at lower levels of the organizational hierarchy; however, senior managers should assist by providing managers at all levels with the necessary information and planning tools.

Responsibility for overall planning and strategy generally lies with senior management; however, managers at all levels of the organizational hierarchy must have the skills necessary to allow them to set goals for their work groups and develop strategies and operational plans that their subordinates can understand and follow in order to achieve those goals. In addition, managers throughout the organization must participate in planning initiatives focusing on coordinating the use of organizational resources so that all of them have access to the resources they need in order to achieve the goals that have been set for their work groups.[37]

A significant influence on the identification and use of "dimensions" for cross-cultural comparisons of management styles was the research conducted by Weihrich to compare management practices in the United States, Japan, and China, work that relied on five dimensions: planning, organizing, staffing, leading, and controlling.[38] The criteria used by Weihrich to compare planning processes included the relative weight given to short- versus long-term planning, the level of participation or involvement by persons at lower levels of the organizational hierarchy, whether decisions were made by one individual at the top of the hierarchy or by consensus or committee, the flow of the decision-making process, and the speed of decision-making and implementation. Weihrich argued that there were significant differences between US and Japanese managers with respect to how they approached planning activities: US managers

---

[37] Lewis, P., S. Goodman, P. Fandt, and J. Michlitsch. 2007. *Management: Challenges for Tomorrow's Leaders*, 6, 5th ed. Mason, OH: Thomson South-Western.

[38] Weihrich, H. March/April 1990. "Management Practices in the United States, Japan and the People's Republic of China." *Industrial Management*, 3–7. For further discussion, see "Comparative Management Studies" in "Management: A Library of Resources for Sustainable Entrepreneurs" prepared and distributed by the Sustainable Entrepreneurship Project (www.seproject.org).

tended to be primarily oriented toward short-term goals and objectives and decisions were generally made solely by the person at the top of the organizational hierarchy and communicated downward; however, in contrast, Japanese managers had a long-term orientation with respect to planning and setting goals and objectives and collective decision-making processes were used to solicit input and achieve consensus among both managers and workers.

## *Manager's Planning Activities and Skills*

- Determining the purpose and overall goals and objectives of the organization
- Mastering the tools and skills necessary to choose among a variety of alternatives for future actions
- Establishing processes for forecasting and coping with future conditions in the organization's external environment
- Developing an overall strategic plan using "SWOT analy-sis" (typically an activity reserved for senior-level managers with inputs from others at lower levels of the organizational hierarchy)
- Identifying and describing the tasks and activities that need to be accomplished to achieve the organizational goals
- Determining the methods to be used for organizing and executing the necessary tasks and activities
- Determining the course of action for undertaking and completing the necessary tasks and activities (i.e., tactical and operational planning)
- Creating and implementing strategies to acquire the resources required in order for the organization to efficiently pursue its goals and objectives
- Establishing procedures for involving employees in planning decisions and communicating decisions and strategies to employees
- Adopting tools and methods (i.e., budgets and schedules) to monitor and measure progress of the organization against goals and milestone established during the planning process

- Developing processes for continuously monitoring changes that will impact pre-existing plans and for avoiding planning approaches that are too rigid and inflexible

## Organizing

Organizing involves "determining the tasks to be done, who will do them, and how those tasks will be managed and coordinated."[39] Managers performing this function must make decisions about organizing the capital, personnel, raw materials, and other resources available to the organization in a manner that is efficient and properly aligned with the activities that must be performed by the organization. In other words, managers must create, implement, and manage an organizational structure that allocates the human resources of the organization in a way that is most effective for achieving the goals and objectives established for the organization. When defined in this manner, organizing includes activities that other scholars, such as Koontz and O'Donnell, have categorized as "staffing" and which include identification of workforce requirements, inventorying the skills of people already available within the organization, recruitment of new employees with skills not otherwise available, placement and promotion, career planning, compensation, and training and development.[40] Organization of activities and relationships within the firm must be addressed continuously by the manager, particularly as the volume of activities increases and the number of employees expands. The organizing function also includes recruiting the right person for each job, making sure that the workforce is trained in the skills necessary to perform their jobs at the level required in order to achieve the plans set for the organization and continuously evaluating the performance of each person to determine whether their activities meet the standards set by management.

---

[39] Lewis, P., S. Goodman, P. Fandt, and J. Michlitsch. 2007. *Management: Challenges for Tomorrow's Leaders*, 6, 5th ed. Mason, OH: Thomson South-Western.
[40] See Weihrich, H. 2004. "Management: Science, Theory, and Practice." In *Essentials of Management: An International Perspective*, eds. Weihrich and Koontz. https://scribd.com/document/106629608/22550642-Management-Science-Theory-and-Practice (accessed December 14, 2018).

There is a wide array of "subtasks" that must be completed when carrying out the organizing function. First of all, the most efficient "work flow" must be identified with eye on making sure that information, resources, and tasks flow logically and efficiently through specific work groups and the organization as a whole.[41] In addition, the scope of authority for managers and reporting channels must be determined and then depicted on some form of organizational chart that everyone can use for reference to understand the "chain of command." The duties and responsibilities of individual jobs should also be determined and described, a process often referred to as "job design." Finally, decisions regarding appropriate grouping of related jobs and activities must be made, which means that managers must make decisions about "departmentalization" and whether groups should be organized based on function, products, geography, or types of customers.

Organizing becomes even more complicated when it is understood that decisions regarding job design have a real impact on how workers feel about their job and their level of motivation. For example, while it might be assumed that narrowing the job content for a particular position, and thus increasing the level of specialization associated with that position, will eventually lead to the holder of that position become extremely proficient in the associated tasks. While this may be good for the organization, the worker may grow dissatisfied and frustrated about his or her inability to achieve personal growth and learn new skills and this may ultimately lead to a drop in organizational commitment, absenteeism, and higher turnover that undermines the gains that the organization believed it achieved from specialization. To avoid these problems, many organizations have tried to balance specialization and work development by focusing on job enrichment programs and use of teams of workers that collaborate on a variety of different tasks; however, these programs do make the organizing function a bit more complicated for the manager.

The decisions made with respect to organizing have a direct and powerful impact on organizational culture. The byproduct of organizing is an organizational structure that defines the environment in which managers

---

[41] Id.

and their subordinates go about their day-to-day activities. If, for example, the structure includes too many levels of hierarchy the culture may soon become one of "frustration" if members are unable to get decisions quickly and feel under-respected since they have not been empowered to take actions on their own. Another problem that should be considered is whether the structure creates too many reporting relationships for employees, thus causing them to be confused about where the instructions should be coming from and whose goals they need to worry about. Finally, a company that has been organized to take advantage of specialized functional skills must be careful not to allow functional parochialism to get in the way of communication and collaboration. It should be noted also that the prevailing values and norms found in the organizational culture will themselves have an impact on the effectiveness and acceptance of organizing decisions. For example, if employees are used to having a high level of autonomy a shift to centralized decision-making will almost inevitably be met with opposition.

Weihrich considered "organizing" and "staffing" as two distinguishable dimensions of management style: the criteria he used to compare organizational practices included an assessment of whether responsibility and accountability was individualistic or collectivist, the degree of formality in the organizational structure, the level of clarity in decision-making responsibilities, and the strength of organizational culture, and the criteria he used to compare staffing practices included procedures for recruiting new employees, factors influencing speed of promotion, performance assessment, training and development, and security of employment.[42] Weihrich noted that organizational structures used by US managers tended to rely on individual responsibility and accountability and those managers preferred formal bureaucratic organizational structures with clear and specific rules and expectations about where decision-making responsibility lied. In Japan, however, organizational structures in Japan were relatively informal in comparison to the United States and based on collective responsibility and accountability. As for staffing practices of the firms in his study, Weihrich found that US companies recruited both

---

[42] Weihrich, H. March/April 1990. "Management Practices in the United States, Japan and the People's Republic of China." *Industrial Management*, pp. 3–7.

from schools and from other firms and employees tended to be more loyal to their professions than their employers and thus were likely to change firms frequently during the course of their careers. Promotions in US firms were based primarily on individual performance and US employees had high expectations with regard to rapid advancement and were subject to frequent performance evaluations with a focus on progress toward attainment of short-term results. In contrast, Japanese firms hired most of their employees directly from school and Japanese employees were intensely loyal to their companies resulting in low mobility between firms. Slow promotion was expected in Japan and newer employees received little or no feedback during their early careers. When feedback was provided it focused on appraisal of long-term performance and training and development was seen as a long-term investment.

## Commanding

Commanding refers to the styles and practices of managers in supervising subordinates as they go about their daily activities. The goal and duty of the manager as a commander is to optimize the return on investment from all of the subordinates in the organization and this means that the manager must be able to inspire the subordinates to carry out their activities in ways that effectively achieve the overall goals and objectives set for the organization. When commanding, managers should communicate organizational goals and policies to subordinates and treat subordinates in a manner that is consistent with organizational policies. Fayol's view was that successful managers communicated clearly and effectively, acted with personal integrity, based their judgments about subordinates on regular audits, and made a sincere effort to know the skills and concerns of their subordinates. Other managerial functions, notably coordinating and controlling, are closely aligned with the commander function. Delegation and communication are important elements of commanding and available managerial tools include regular and effective meetings and conferences.

The "commanding" function has often been described in other ways, such as "directing" and "leading" and, in fact, there is obviously overlap between the skills associated with commanding and those typically associated with being an effective organizational "leader." An important distinction is that the leader of the organization, such as the CEO, must develop a message and style that reaches out across hundreds or thousands of employees, most of whom the leader will never meet personally. In contrast, the manager that Fayol was speaking to is seeing his or her subordinates regularly and continuously and an important measure of that manager's effectiveness is his or her ability to motivate subordinates to invest their efforts to achieve the goals set by the organization as a whole and the manager specifically. The modern manager can rarely expect to lead simply by issuing orders and must now be versed in the analytical and communications tools that have been developed through research on the personalities and values of subordinates and how they feel about the manager-subordinated relationship. Managers may often have to use different directive styles depending on the circumstances and must also be mindful that while they are vested with the power of their positions that power must be used effectively in order for it to have any value for the organization.

Weihrich's comparative study of management styles of US, Japanese, and Chinese managers included "leading" as one of the dimensions and the criteria he used to compare leadership practices included the preferred leadership style (e.g., directive or paternalistic), an assessment of the manager's role with respect to leadership of the group, attitudes toward confrontation and group harmony, and the flow of communication.[43] According to Weihrich, the leadership style relied upon by managers in the United States tended to be strong and directive with the senior manager acting as the decision maker and communications flowing top-down. Individualism complicated the task of managers as leaders in the United States and face-to-face confrontations were common as leaders attempted to clarify their decisions and expectations. In contrast, Japanese managers and workers preferred a paternalistic style and Japanese managers saw themselves as members of the group with a responsibility to guide communications and interaction within the group. When leading Japanese managers emphasized cooperation and harmony, sought to avoid confrontation, and encouraged bottom-up communication.

---

[43] Id.

# Coordinating

Coordinating refers to the actions taken by the manager to unify and harmonize the activities of the various departments and other units within the organization so that those activities complement each other and the overall workflow within the organization remains balanced and efficient. For example, coordination among the sales, purchasing, and manufacturing departments is essential to ensuring that a sufficient volume of product is available to meet the immediate needs of willing customers and to guarding against excess inventories of finished product that cannot be sold and which create unnecessary costs and losses for the organization. One specific method for facilitating coordination recommended by Fayol was scheduling weekly meetings among the heads of various departments to discuss and resolve issues of common interest and concern. Most commentators on management agree that coordination is an important activity but often omit it as a separate functional category on the basis that it is a necessary component of the other functions and thus already covered by activities such as commanding and controlling.

# Controlling

Controlling refers to the actions taken by managers to ensure that the activities conducted within the organization conform to the organizational goals and objectives and policies established by the organization. In other words, managers control in order to keep things going "according to plan" and make sure that subordinate adhere to the principles established through the other managerial functions (e.g., work is conducted in a manner consistent with the organizational structure established by the manager). Control methods include observation of the activities of departments and individual subordinates, measurement of performance, and reports of deviations from organizational goals and policies accompanied by appropriate remedial actions. While the term "controlling" is often associated with "manipulation" and thus has a negative connotation, in this context the process is not intended to unnecessarily interfere in the way that jobs are performed or create stress or discomfort for subordinates but rather is concerned with the responsibility of the manager to ensure that his or her decisions in fulfilling the other functions are leading to the expected leading to the desired results.

Controlling is an integral part of the commanding function and is also closely related to the manager's planning responsibilities. In fact, the foundation for a manager's controlling activities is actually the creation of a plan for the resources under the manager's control accompanied by performance goals and objectives that can be measured during the controlling process. Barnett has explained that controlling consists of three steps: "establishing performance standards, comparing actual performance against standards, and taking corrective action when necessary."[44] Many goals and objectives set by an organization can be defined in monetary terms, such as revenues, expenses, and profits; however, other non-monetary performance standards must be used to assess key organizational activities such as the volume of units produced, the percentage of defective products, and quantitative measures of customer satisfaction. Managers must be familiar with a variety of reports and other tools in order to become proficient "controllers," including budgets, financial statements, sales reports, manufacturing reports, customer satisfaction surveys, performance audits, and formal performance appraisals of individual workers. While financial-based goals and objectives require a great deal of attention for the "controller," Barnett cautions that "managers must also control production/operations processes, procedures for delivery of services, compliance with company policies, and many other activities within the organization."

Controlling is also related to the manager's coordination function and managers analyzing deviations from standards uncovered in a performance assessment must seek a clear understanding of where responsibility for the problem actually rests within the organizational structure that the

---

[44] Barnett, T. n.d. "Encyclopedia of Management: Management Functions." https://referenceforbusiness.com/management/Log-Mar/Management-Functions.html (accessed December 14, 2018). While "corrective action" certainly includes improvements in the efforts being made to achieve the original objectives, corrections also include adjustments to the goals and/or related strategy to take into account new information about the current situation confronting the organization or work group.

manager has created, particularly when the standard in question relies on coordination and cooperation between two or more employees, teams, or departments. For example, while low levels of customer satisfaction can reasonably become an issue for members of the group assigned responsibility for customer support to explain the manager should be sure that the performance of other groups is not contributing to the problem. As part of his or her analysis, the manager should be sure that parts normally controlled by other groups are available to customer support when needed to address warranty issues and that the company's communications and information systems are working efficiently so that word of customer issues is getting to the support team in a timely fashion and the team is able to respond to customers within the period that the company has promised.

The criteria used by Weihrich to compare control practices among US, Japanese, and Chinese managers included the locus of control (i.e., senior manager/group leader or peers), focus of control (i.e., individual or group performance), the importance of placing blame or "saving face," and the use of group improvement strategies such as quality control circles.[45] He argued that US managers tended to rely on formal control rules and procedures formulated and disseminated at the top of the organizational hierarchy and focusing on individual performance to identify persons responsible for any failure to meet organizational goals and objectives (i.e., "fix blame"). In contrast, the control systems established in Japanese firms relied heavily on group responsibility for group performance and "saving face" rather than "fixing blame" was important to maintenance of harmony and respect for the Japanese.

---

[45] Weihrich, H. March/April 1990. "Management Practices in the United States, Japan and the People's Republic of China." *Industrial Management*, pp. 3–7.

# CHAPTER 2

# Management Skills

## Introduction

Researchers and commentators have attempted to identify the skills, motivations, and behaviors that managers and administrators must have in order to effectively carry out their duties and responsibilities. The search has led to a plethora of suggestions and the challenge is to devise methods for assisting both new and experienced managers in identifying, acquiring, and practicing the tools they need in order to be successful in their managerial roles. There is no single answer since the particular skills that a specific manager may need will vary depending on whether he or she is engaged in "general" or "functional" management and where the manager fits into the overall organizational hierarchy, and other situational factors certainly play an important part in determining what might be "effective management" in a specific context. Moreover, success in formal management education does not guarantee that someone will be a strong manager and learning from experience, including mistakes, is necessary to improve existing skills and acquire new skills.

Researchers such as Fayol and Mintzberg focused their attention on the functions and roles of managers and the implicit message was that managerial skill development should concentrate on building the capacity to be effective in performing these functions and roles.[1] Mintzberg's efforts to identify some of the distinguishing characteristics of managerial work, which ultimately led to the creation of his model of "managerial roles," were accompanied by his assessment that effective managers must recognize and master a number of important "managerial skills,"

---

[1] For discussion of views of Fayol and Mintzberg on the functions and roles of managers see "Management Roles and Activities" prepared and distributed by the Sustainable Entrepreneurship Project (www.seproject.org).

including development and nurturing of peer relationships (i.e., liaison contacts), negotiation and conflict resolution skills, the ability to motivate and inspire subordinates, establishment and maintenance of information networks, the ability to communication effectively when disseminating information, and the ability to make decisions in conditions of extreme ambiguity and allocate resources, and he argued that the entire process of identifying the various managerial roles and related skills, while not guaranteeing that a manager will be effectiveness and successful, provided a framework for setting priorities and establishing a managerial training regimen. Mintzberg's work provided support for managerial skills posited by others: the need to deal with an unrelenting pace of activities and decisions, the need to cope with complexity; the need to manage the scarce resources of time and attention; preferences for verbal media; and the need to create and nurture communication relationships with superiors, outsiders, and subordinates. A general review of the literature expands the list of desired managerial attributes, activities, and skills to include an even wider range of things such as leadership, people focus, human resource management, communications, and interpersonal skills, conflict resolution, information processing, the ability to make decisions under ambiguous conditions, resource allocation, entrepreneurship, and introspection.

Boyatzis identified the following set of "managerial competencies" based on his "critical incident" research: efficiency orientation, particularly focusing on objectives, tasks, and achievements and setting challenging goals and supporting appropriate planning; concern with impact and demonstrating a significant interest in power and its symbols; proactivity, including a strong belief in self-control and self-driven action; self-confidence and a belief in self, values and ideas that translates into confident and decisive action; oral presentation skills and the ability to use effective language, modes of speech and body language; conceptualization, including the ability to use inductive reasoning and creative thinking to identify patterns and relationships and create models and symbols to communicate these concepts; diagnostic use of concepts, particularly the ability to concerts the products of conceptualization into practical tools and ideas to address specific problems and opportunities; use of socialized power, including the ability to develop networks of relationships that can be used to achieve specific ends; and managing group processes, particularly "team building" around common goals and objectives, development of group roles and the capacity to create ways for people to work together effectively.[2]

Traits and characteristics have been a popular method of evaluating the potential for effective and successful leadership. For example, Ghiselli highlighted the traits of initiative, self-assurance, individuality, supervisory ability, and intelligence.[3] Other researchers identified numerous other traits, many of which were difficult to define with specificity and sometimes incapable to being acquired, such as "personality," "image," "charisma," "energetic," "worldly," and even height. Another approach focused on "behaviors" of effective and successful managers, a concept similar to listing functions and roles, and the most commonly cited of these included controlling the organization's environment, similar to the "proactivity" mentioned earlier; organizing and controlling, including the use of information and communications channels; information handling; providing for professional growth and development of self and subordinates; motivation; conflict resolution; and strategic problem solving and decision-making.[4] Finally, Miner and Smith tried to explain that "motivation to manage" influenced managerial effectiveness and could be described by the following categories: authority acceptance (i.e., desire and willingness to accept authority of superiors); competitive games and situations, both of which were based on a desire to engage in competition with peers; assertiveness; imposing wishes (i.e., desire to tell others what to do and to influence through sanctions); distinctiveness (i.e., a desire to stand out from the group); and a desire to carry out the routine functions associated with managerial responsibilities.[5]

---

[2] Boyatsis, R. 1982. *The Competent Manager*. New York, NY: John Wiley and Sons.

[3] Ghiselli, E. 1963. "Managerial Talent." *American Psychologist* 18, pp. 631–42.

[4] Morse, J., and F. Wagner. 1978. "Measuring the Process of Managerial Effectiveness." *Academy of Management Journal* 16, pp. 23–35. Morse and Wagner argued that these six behaviors explained greater than 50 percent of managerial effectiveness.

[5] Miner, J., and N. Smith. 1982. "Decline and Stabilization of Managerial Motivation Over a 20-Year Period." *Journal of Applied Psychology* 43, pp. 297–305.

Clearly there is no lack of variety in ideas about what should be in a manager's "skill set" and it is useful to try and simplify the analysis so that practicing managers have a better idea of what might be expected of them and educators can determine the appropriate goals and objectives of management training activities. As discussed below, Cameron and Whetten were able to distill the most commonly cited ideas of the research community down to a fairly manageable list. Other commentators suggested that effective managers are competent with respect to technical, human, and conceptual skills, a list that is sometimes expanded to include design and political skills.[6] The views of business and management educators can be understood by the recommendations of the American Assembly of Collegiate Schools of Business that curricula in business schools should focus on helping students develop skills in areas such as leadership, self-objectivity, analytic and thinking, behavioral flexibility, oral and written communications, and personal impact.

## Katz's Skills of Effective Administrators

Katz was among the first to focus on the important problem of attempting to identify the skills that a person required in order to be an effective and successful manager. In a legendary article published in 1955, Katz introduced his model of "management skills" that was based on three categories: technical skills, human skills, and conceptual skills.[7] Katz's model has been widely accepted in the management literature, particularly in textbooks; however, there have been some attempts to expand the number of categories. For example, the discussion below includes a fourth

---

[6] See, e.g., Robbins, S., and P. Hunsaker. 1996. *Training in Interpersonal Skills*, 1–32, 2nd ed. Upper Saddle River, NJ: Prentice Hall; Mintzberg, H. 1974. "The Manager's Job: Folklore and Fact." *Harvard Business Review* 53, pp. 49–71; Katz, R. 1974. "Skills of an Effective Administrator." *Harvard Business Review* 52, pp. 90–102; and Pavett, C., and A. Lau. 1983. "Managerial Work: The Influence of Hierarchical Level and Functional Specialty." *Academy Management Journal* 21, pp. 170–77.

[7] See Katz, R. January-February 1955. "Skills of an Effective Administrator." *Harvard Business Review*, pp. 33–42; and Katz, R. September-October, 1974. "Retrospective Commentary." *Harvard Business Review*, pp. 101–02.

category, referred to as "design skills," which was suggested by Weihrich and Koontz.[8] While not included in the discussion below, commentators such as Pavett and Lau have lobbied for the inclusion of "political skills," which would include the ability of a manager to gain power and influence within the organization.[9]

## Technical Skills

Technical skills include knowledge of, and proficiency in, activities that involve methods, processes, and procedures. Technical skills in a particular field are developed and maintained through the use of various tools, techniques, and procedures that are specific to that field. For example, a worker engaged in mechanical activities will carry out his or her activities by using specific mechanical tools and the manager of that worker must have the technical skills and background to be able to instruct the worker about how to use those tools. Similarly, a manager or supervisor in the accounting area must be able to advise subordinates about accounting principles and practices and answer any technical questions that they might have with respect to the way they are expected to carry out their duties and responsibilities. Technical skills tend to be most important for managers at lower levels of the organizational hierarchy and tend to become less important as one moves up the hierarchy through middle management to senior management.

---

[8] Weihrich, H., and H. Koontz. 1993. *Management: A Global Perspective*, 10th ed. New York, NY: McGraw-Hill. Design skills are similar to the "diagnostic skills" suggested by Griffin in Griffin, R. 2008. *Fundamentals of Management*, 6th ed. Mason, OH: South-Western Cengage Learning. The discussion of the various management skills in the following sections is adapted from Weihrich, H. 2004. "Management: Science, Theory, and Practice." In *Essentials of Management: An International Perspective*, eds. H. Weihrich and H. Koontz, https://scribd.com/document/106629608/22550642-Management-Science-Theory-and-Practice (accessed December 14, 2018).

[9] Pavett, C., and A. Lau. 1983. "Managerial Work: The Influence of Hierarchical Level and Functional Specialty." *Academy of Management Journal* 26, no. 1, pp. 170–77.

# Human Skills

As the name implies, "human" skills are "people" skills and include the ability to work effectively with others, including subordinates and persons at the same or higher levels in the organizational hierarchy, and the ability of a manager to understand his or her own needs, strengths, weaknesses, and motivations. Specific human skills include development of self-awareness; the ability to cope with personal stress; the ability to coach, counsel, and motivate others; conflict management; and the ability to empower others to perform their jobs and improve their own skills. Someone with effective human skills is able to encourage cooperation and teamwork and the managers and administrators with the best human skills are those that are able to create an environment in which subordinates feel secure and empowered to express their opinions about the best way to organize work activities. Human skills are essential for every manager, regardless of where he or she is located in the organizational hierarchy; however, the frequency and content of interactions with others within the organization will obviously vary depending on the manager's position and duties.

# Conceptual Skills

Conceptual skills incorporate the skills associated with the ability to see and comprehend the "big picture," including recognizing and analyzing the significant elements of a particular situation and how they fit together. In other words, conceptual skills are the ability to analyze complex situations.[10] Not surprisingly, conceptual skills are most important to, and most frequently used by, members of the senior management group. For example, conceptual skills are needed by senior managers seeking to understand how the various different units of a business related to one another and fit within the overall organizational design of the business. Specific conceptual skills that are particularly important include planning and strategizing, decision-making, organizing, and controlling.

---

[10] Lewis, P., S. Goodman, P. Fandt, and J. Michlitsch. 2007. *Management: Challenges for Tomorrow's Leaders*, 10, 5th ed. Mason, OH: Thomson South-Western.

# Design Skills

Design skills, the category suggested by Weihrich and Koontz, complement conceptual skills and focus on how a manager or administrator helps the organization cope with its environment by identifying and solving problems in ways that will benefit the organization. Weihrich and Koontz argued that it was not enough for a manager or administrator to use his or her conceptual skills to identify problems or threats in the organizational environment and in order for the manager or administrator to provide value he or she must be able to come up with a practical solution. They analogized those activities to what a good "design engineer" does and it is reasonable to look at the "problem solving" process as involving the various elements of organizational design, including setting the appropriate strategy, selecting the most efficient organizational structure, identifying the necessary human resources, and acquiring and implementing the technology best suited for solving the problem. Given what is involved with design skills, including input into the organizational design process, it is not surprising that design skills, like conceptual skills, are most important at the senior management level.

# Cameron and Whetten's Skills of Effective Managers

## Characteristics of Effective Managers

Most people assuming managerial positions in their organization want more than just status and truly want to be effective in their roles and contribute to improving organizational performance. In order for this to happen it is necessary for managers to have some idea about the experiences of others and a sense of which management practices have been adopted and used by effective managers. Surveys conducted around the world are beginning to uncover universal characteristics of managers who empower their subordinates and strengthen their organizations: self-awareness; creative problem solving abilities; communication skills; effective delegation, and ability to facilitate and oversee joint decision-making; beneficial use of power to influence; conflict management skills; ability to monitor information and use and distribute it for continuous improvement; ability to set the right targets, monitor progress, and take appropriate actions to make changes when targets and outcomes are not aligned; and a focus on hiring and keeping the best employees and promoting and reward employees based on their performance and contributions.

As part of their efforts to create a model curriculum for "teaching management skills," which are discussed in more detail below, Cameron and Whetten took on the task of identifying exactly what those skills might be.[11] They argued that "skills" are different from characteristics and activities often associated with management, such as personality traits and motivations and two other issues already discussed earlier: functions and roles. They believed that skills "include cognitive knowledge of how to perform and action, but they involve more than just knowledge itself."[12] They finally settled on the following definition of "management skills": "[a] management skill involves a sequential pattern of behaviors performed in order to achieve a designed outcome."[13] Using such a definition eliminated personal traits (e.g., honesty and loyalty), since they are not defined by a specific, sequential set of behaviors, and also eliminated functions and roles because they involve a variety of patterns of behaviors.

Cameron and Whetten went on propose a list of the skills that are performed by "effective" managers, a process that began with their own study of managers at various levels of a number of public and private organizations and then was supplemented with a comparison of their results with the findings of other scholars who had proposed their own collection of characteristics of effective managers.[14] The result was the

---

[11] Cameron, K., and D. Whetten, "A Model for Teaching Management Skills." *Organizational Behavior Teaching Journal* 8, no. 2, pp. 21–27.

[12] Id. at p. 22.

[13] Id.

[14] The results of their own research were summarized in detail in Whetten, D., and K. Cameron. 1984. *Developing Management Skills*, Glenview, IL: Scott, Foresman and Company. Other scholars whose works were considered included Boyatsis, R. 1982. *The Competent Manager*. New York, NY: John Wiley and Sons; Ghiselli, E. 1963. "Managerial Talent." *American Psychologist* 18, no. 10, pp. 631–42; Livingston, J. 1971. "Myth of the Well Educated Manager." *Harvard Business Review* 49, pp. 79–89; Miner, J. 1973. "The Real Crunch in Managerial Manpower." *Harvard Business Review* 51, no. 6, pp. 146–58; and Mintzberg, H. 1975. "The Manager's Job: Folklore and Fact." *Harvard Business Review* 53, no. 4, pp. 49–71.

following list of both personal and interpersonal skills that was limited to characteristics that had "trainable behavioral components"[15]:

- Self-awareness (personality, values, needs, and cognitive style)
- Managing personal stress (time management, personal goals, and activity balance)
- Creative problem solving (divergent thinking, conceptual blocks, and redefining problems)
- Establishing supportive communication (listening, empathy, and counseling)
- Improving employee performance and motivating others (needs/expectations, rewards, and timing)
- Effective delegation and joint decision-making (assigning tasks, evaluating performance, and autonomous versus joint decision-making)
- Gaining power and influence (sources of power, converting power to influence, and beneficial use (not abuse) of power
- Managing conflict (sources of conflict assertiveness and sensitivity and handling criticism)
- Improving group decision-making (chairing meetings, avoiding pitfalls of bad meetings, and making effective presentations)

### Best Practices for Managers Emerge from International Study

Bloom and Van Reenen completed an exhaustive international study of patterns of management and productivity based on almost 6,000 interviews conducted at large samples of firms in 17 countries including the United States, Great Britain, a number of countries in Western Europe, Brazil, China, and Japan. The premise of their study was that effective management required knowledge, selection and use of "best practices" in three broad areas: "monitoring management," which involves how well managers monitor what goes on inside their firms and use this

---

[15] Cameron, K., and D. Whetten. 1983. "A Model for Teaching Management Skills." *Organizational Behavior Teaching Journal* 8, no. 2, pp. 21–27, 22.

information for continuous improvement; "targets management," which involves setting the right targets for the firm, tracking the right outcomes for the firms and then taking appropriate action when targets and outcomes are inconsistent; and "incentives management," which involves promoting and rewarding employees based on performance and trying to hire and keep the best employees. Using the dimensions employed by Bloom and Van Reenen in their survey, it is possible to suggest the following guiding principles for effective management in each of the areas mentioned earlier:

Monitoring Management:

- Effective managers are enthusiastic about introducing and adopting the full range of modern manufacturing techniques (e.g., just-in-time delivery from suppliers, automation, flexible manpower, support systems, attitudes, and behavior), and do so not because others are using them but because they can be linked to meeting business objectives like reducing costs and improving quality.
- Effective managers actively seek out process improvements for continuous improvement as part of a normal business process rather than waiting until problems arise.
- Effective managers continually track performance and communicate the result to all members of the group as opposed to relying on ad hoc and incomplete tracking systems.
- Effective managers review performance continually with an expectation of continuous improvement as opposed to infrequent performance reviews are based only on a success/failure scale.
- Effective managers ensure that in review/performance conversations the purpose, data, agenda, and follow-up steps (like coaching) are clear to all parties.

Targets Management:

- Effective managers establish and rely on a balance of financial and non-financial targets.
- Effective managers establish goals that are based on shareholder value, not accounting value, and which are defined

in a way that works through business units and ultimately is connected to individual performance expectations.

- Effective managers avoid focusing mainly on the short term and instead visualize short-term targets as a "staircase" toward their main focus on long-term goals.
- Effective managers establish goals that are demanding yet attainable for all parts of the firm and avoid setting goals for "sacred cows" areas of the firm that are too easy to achieve.
- Effective managers establish performance measures that are well-defined, clearly communicated, and publicly available.

Incentives Management:

- In well-managed organizations senior managers are evaluated and held accountable for attracting, retaining, and developing talent throughout the organization.
- Well-managed organizations do a better job than their competitors in offering strong reasons for talented people to join them.
- Effective managers establish and enforce reward systems in which rewards are related to performance and effort rather than distributed equally irrespective of the performance level.
- Effective managers establish and enforce promotion systems that emphasize active identification, development, and promotion of top performers and avoid promotion based mainly on tenure.
- Effective managers make it clear that failure to achieve agreed objectives carry consequences, which can include re-training or re-assignment to other jobs.
- Effective managers ensure that poor performers are re-trained and/or moved into different roles or out of the company as soon as the weakness is identified.
- Well-managed organizations do whatever it takes to retain top talent when they look likely to leave.

While many of the suggestions are not "new news," the Bloom and Van Reenen study was important as a source of empirical confirmation that firms and managers that embraced the management practices described earlier would likely be rewarded with better performance on a wide range of dimensions: they were larger, more productive, grew faster, and had higher survival rates.

*Sources*: N. Bloom and J. Van Reenen, "Why Do Management Practices Differ across Firms and Countries," *Journal of Economic Perspectives*, 24(1) (Winter 2010), 203-224. A full set of questions for each dimension appears in N. Bloom and J. Van Reenen, "Measuring and Explaining Management Practices Across Firms and Countries," Centre for Economic Performance Discussion Paper 716 (2006). See the chapter on "Cross-Cultural Studies of Management Practices" in "Management: A Library of Resources for Sustainable Entrepreneurs" prepared and distributed by the Sustainable Entrepreneurship Project (www.seproject.org).

## Harris' Multi-Factor Analysis of Characteristics of Effective Managers

Harris argued that there was really no single and definitive answer as to "what makes an effective manager" and that effectiveness and success depends on a variety of factors including the management theory in use; the organizational context, including the form of organizational structure, organizational culture, and the position and level of the manager in the organizational hierarchy; the personality characteristics of the manager; and the manager's cognitive skills based on several different measures of intelligence and creativity.[16] She observed that since there was "no universal definition of *the* effective manager, characteristics must be matched to the context and situation to be effective."

Harris noted that conceptions and theories of the role of the manager, and thus the characteristics of what might normally be considered effective management, have evolved as time has gone by and it was possible and useful to place management theories into four time periods beginning with "pre-scientific," before the beginning of the Industrial Revolution in the 1880s, and then continuing with "classical" (1880s through 1920s), "neo-classical" (early 1930s through 1950s), and "modern" (beginning

---

[16] Harris' discussion was adapted from Bowditch, J., and A. Buono. 1994. *A Primer on Organizational Behavior*, 3rd ed. New York, NY: John Wiley & Sons.

around 1960).[17] The role of the manager suggested by each of these theories varied depending upon the underlying assumptions regarding factors such as the nature of society, the locus and nature of work, management and organizational theory, assumptions about human nature, and the focus of managerial control. Changes in technology and available resource also played an important role in the evolution of management styles and practices and principles of organizational design.

During the pre-scientific period workers had little or no mobility and thus were tied to jobs that they often believed were part of their preordained stations in life. As such, the responsibilities of managers were largely confined to keeping workers in line and little attention was paid to motivational techniques or caring about the worker's well-being or career development. Classical management theory came into fashion as machines became a large part of the workplace and theorists urged managers to view their workers as extensions of the machines and focus their efforts on developing and using reward and punishment techniques that would control and behavior of employees. While this approach was accepted for decades, mechanistic treatment of workers, which often included abusive and authoritarian practices, eventually came under sharp criticism and neo-classical theorists working and writing around 1930 called for managers to respect the human aspects of their employees and use management techniques that were based on creating and maintaining employee social systems rather than on controlling behavior.

Harris described modern management theories, which began to take shape in the early 1960s, as emphasizing "facilitation of employee development" and based on the premise that organizations were "systems composed of mutually interrelated and independent variables" and were also part of a system that was linked with the external environment. All this meant that changes initiated by managers in one part of the organization would trigger changes in other parts of the organization that needed to be taken into account. Managers thus needed to cope with greater uncertainty and also needed to deal with rapid changes in the organization's

---

[17] Id. at p. 1. See also Bowditch, J., and A. Buono. 1994. *A Primer on Organizational Behavior*, 8. New York, NY: John Wiley & Sons. (Figure: Historical Perspective of the Evolution of Management and Organization).

external environment due to factors such as technological progress, globalization, cynicism and diversity in the workplace and demands of customers (e.g., the "quality movement" influenced production processes and managerial goals and objectives). Modern management theories also include a sharper focus on identifying and acknowledging differences in the needs and motives of individual workers with regarding to their jobs and career development.

According to Harris there were three major developments associated with the rise of modern management theory that significantly changed the roles and responsibilities of managers and influenced the behaviors expected of them in order to be successful[18]:

- Management science, which was explained by Harris as being the application of quantitative techniques to management and organizational problems. Among other things, managers were tasked with integrating computers into their analysis of operational problems and implementing wide-ranging processes such as just-in-time production and total quality management.
- Systems theory, which called for managers to understand their organizations as a set of mutually dependent subsystems: task subsystem (i.e., the tasks that actually have to be completed); administrative/structural subsystem (i.e., the formal organizational structure); individual subsystem (i.e., the people within the organization and their specific nature and characteristics); and "emergent" subsystem (i.e., the informal organization). Among other things, systems theory requires that managers pay more attention to the people that work for them and their needs with regard to satisfaction, understanding their places in the organization and development.
- Contingency theory, which was based on the premise that there were few, if any, universal management approaches and the actions of managers needed to be tailored to the

---

[18] Id. at pp. 2–3.

specific situation (i.e., the unique then-current environmental conditions and internal factors). Acceptance of contingency theory implied that effective management involved the ability to assess the situation and context and select and apply the appropriate managerial style and practices.

Another important factor that needs to be taken into account in determining the most effective type of managerial style is the structure of the organization. Harris commented that "[a] trend line of future career characteristics can be drawn using three key ideas about organization structure: organization structure dictates core managerial competencies, different organization structures require a different mix of managerial competencies, and organizational structure dictates how careers are managed."[19] Arguing that effective management characteristics must be aligned with the structure in use by the organization at a particular time, Harris provided the an overview of what researchers had found to be the most effective managerial characteristics for each of the most popular types of organizational structures[20]:

- In **functional** structures, managers typically spend most of their careers in one department focusing on developing their skills in a single technical competency. As such, technical skills are most important to them for career advancement and they rarely are exposed to learning managerial skills unless and until they progress to the top of their function.
- **Divisional** structures support the creation of independent business units, all with their own full complement of functional resources. A prospective manager in a divisional structure is more likely to have exposure to issues that cut across functional lines and thus will be able to develop both technical and commercial skills and competencies.

[19] Id. at p. 3. Adapted from Allred, B., C. Snow, and R. Miles. 1996. "Characteristics of Managerial Careers in the 21st Century." *Academy of Management Executive* 10, no. 4, p. 17.
[20] Id. at pp. 3–9.

- In **matrix** structures employees must have both technical skills to progress in their own functional department and commercial skills to contribute to cross-functional project or program groups. Harris suggested that commercial skills are even more important to prospective mangers in a matrix structure than in a divisional structure since individuals working in a matrix organization are exposed to many different parts of the larger organization rather than being largely confined to their own business unit.
- Harris described **network** organizations as relying on linkages with "independent firms to provide the critical expertise needed for specific projects or products" and noted that managers working within this type of structure not only needed both technical and commercial skills for work inside their firm but also collaborative knowledge and abilities for work with outside partners that included three particular types of relationships and skills: referral skills, partnering skills, and relationship management.
- Harris suggested that the use of **teams**, and creation of team-based organizations, was a specialized form of the network organization that called for managers to employ a mix of a wide range of team- and task-based managerial skills. One commentator suggested that managers of effective team are adept as an internal consultant, visionary, experimenter, coach, and educator.[21] Other researchers argued that team managers must have skills and abilities with respect to advising, innovating, promoting, developing, organizing, producing, inspecting, and maintaining standards and values, and must also be able to develop those skills among team members.[22]
- Harris described **cellular** organizations as being composed of multiple "cells," which can be a team, a business unit, or a

[21] See Antonioni, D. 1994. "Managerial Roles for Effective Team Leadership." *Supervisory Management* 39, no. 5, p. 3.
[22] Margerison, C., and D. McCann. 1995. "Team Tasks and Management Development." *American Journal of Management Development* 1, no. 1, pp. 22–25.

firm) with specific responsibilities to the entire organization, and which is fluid enough to continually reorganize in order to meet the changing needs of the organization. Managers in cellular organizations will need to have knowledge-based technical skills; however, they will likely need to assume more personal responsibility for acquiring and maintaining those skills and be more proactive in seeking opportunities to develop their careers. As with matrix and network organizations, commercial skills will be essential for managers in cellular organizations. Project management and collaborative skills will also be important in cellular organizations since project teams will generally be the organizing unit.

As is the case with leadership, management takes on a different meaning depending upon the organizational level at which the manager is operating.[23] Harris described models of managerial tasks and responsibilities that focused on similarities and differences depending on where the manager fell within the following multi-level model:

- **Executive-level** management responsibilities typically emphasized concern for "systems leadership," including planning for periods extending out many years into the future. Executives needed to be have a good grasp of the tools necessary for effective strategizing.
- **Middle-level** managers were more involved with "organizational leadership," which was described as the process of integrating the goals established at the executive level into the day-to-day operations of the organization.
- **Front-line** managers, the supervisors working directly with workers at the production and service levels, were responsible for ensuring that all the necessary day-to-day tasks relating to achievement of goals were completed.

---

[23] Harris, C. 2010. *Characteristics of Effective Managers*, 8. Harris' discussion was adapted from Bowditch, J., and A. Buono. 1994. *A Primer on Organizational Behavior*, 3rd ed. New York, NY: John Wiley & Sons.

Harris commented that as a manager moves from front-line responsibilities up toward executive leadership, he or she must learn how to cope with greater complexity and develop and broader strategies that extend for longer time periods. Harris noted that career progress requires a capacity to deal with changes in complexity and that not everyone will be successful at each level. For example, excellent front-line supervisors who are consistently able to motive their workers may struggle when asked to take on systems and organizational leadership activities. In turn, the CEO may bring exceptional vision and clarity of purpose to the organization but fail miserably if asked to oversee a small part of the production process.

Managerial style and effectiveness is also influenced by individual characteristics of the manager including personality and intelligence.[24] Use of personality measures to distinguish between good and poor managers has become quite popular and indications are that certain characteristics are regularly associated with people who are considered to be successful and effective managers. Researchers using the Occupational Personality Questionnaire found that the best managers were creative people who could generate ideas and had a flair for ingenuity, who were intellectually curious and enjoyed the opportunity to deal with complex and abstract matters, and who enjoyed analyzing, as opposed to simply measuring data and applying the analysis to solving problems.[25] In another survey, researchers found that "ideal" managers were strong with respect to continuous learning and sociability and scored poorly with respect to "remaining even tempered" and "eagerness to please." In turn, common characteristics of poorer managers included "remaining even tempered" and "conforming."[26]

---

[24] Id. at pp. 9–10.

[25] Id. at p. 9 (citing Kinder, A., and I. Robertson. 1994. "Do you have the Personality to be a Leader?" *Leadership and Organization Development Journal* 15, no. 1, pp. 3–12).

[26] Id. (citing Holland, B. April 1998. "Preliminary Report: Redesigning the Hogan Descriptive Adjective Inventory." *Presentation at 44th Annual Conference of Southwest Psychological Association*, New Orleans).

As for "intelligence," Harris noted that researchers believed it to be concept relevant to predicting and assessing managerial effectiveness; however, the appropriate assessment likely needed to go beyond "traditional" intelligence tests ("IQ") and include three key elements of what Sternberg referred to as "managerial intelligence"[27]:

- Analytical intelligence, which consisted of meta-components (planning, monitoring, and problem solving), performance components (execution of solutions derived from meta-components), and knowledge acquisition (skills relating learning how to solve problems)
- Practical intelligence (i.e., "common sense"), which includes the ability to adapt to and shape environments and is often measured by accessing "tacit knowledge" (described by Harris as "action-oriented knowledge acquired without direct help from others")
- Creative intelligence, which included resources such as intellectual ability (particularly the ability to think "outside the box"), knowledge, styles of thinking, personality, motivation, and environment

Harris noted that certain areas referred earlier, such as tacit knowledge and creativity, appeared to be particularly important for managers needed to deal with increasingly complex problems and thus required further study. Accepting the utility of the concept of managerial intelligence is one thing; however, the challenge for managers is mixing and using all three forms of intelligence, accepting that there is no "one best way," and working to identify individual strengths and weaknesses and then exploiting the strengths and working around weaknesses (e.g., seeking training for personal improvement or bringing on personnel who can provide the missing skills).[28]

---

[27] Id. at pp. 9–10 (citing Sternberg, R. 1997. "Managerial Intelligence: Why IQ isn't Enough." *Journal of Management* 23, no. 3, pp. 475–95).

[28] Id. at p. 10.

## Management Competency Models

Harris observed that insights regarding characteristics and behaviors of effective managers can be derived from a review of various management competency models and surveys designed to gather information from experts in order to create a profile of an effective manager.[29] For example, McNary argued that "the main goal for a manager is to optimize the system of interdependent components through cooperation to foster organization success" and suggested that effective managers solicit informal feedback from, and engage in coaching of, the subordinates in order to foster their intrinsic motivation; employ statistical and analytical thinking when making decisions; focus on a "systems view" with a particular emphasis on improvement and innovation; and pay close attention to development and maintenance of external relationships with customers and suppliers.[30] Results of a survey of managers of leading-edge companies reported by Allred et al. predicted that future managerial careers would be based on knowledge-based technical specialization, cross-functional and international experience, competencies in collaborative leadership, self-management skills and, finally, development of certain personality traits such as flexibility, integrity, and trustworthiness.[31]

Davis et al. reported that Personnel Decisions, Inc. had developed assessment tools for gauging effective management behaviors that focused on measuring the following factors deemed to relevant to performance by managers at all levels in the organization[32]:

- Administrative skills: Structuring of activities and coordination of resources including specific skills with respect

---

[29] Id. at pp. 10–11.

[30] Id. at p. 10 (citing McNary, L. 1997. "The System of Profound Knowledge: A Revised Profile of Managerial Leadership." *Leadership and Organization Development Journal* 18, no. 5, p. 229).

[31] Id. at p. 10 (citing Allred, B., C. Snow, and R. Miles. 1996. "Characteristics of Managerial Careers in the 21st Century." *Academy of Management Executive* 10, no. 4, p. 17).

[32] Id. at p. 11 (citing Davis, B., L. Hellervik, and J. Sheard, eds. 1989. *Successful Manager's Handbook*. Minneapolis, MN: Personnel Decisions, Inc.).

to planning, organizing, and personal organization and time management

- Leadership skills: Selection and use of leadership styles, ability to motivate others, group management skills, delegation and control, staffing and coaching, and development of others
- Interpersonal skills: Human relations skills, negotiation skills, and conflict resolution
- Communication skills: Oral and written communications skills and ability to disseminate information and listen to ideas and feedback from others
- Personal adaptability skills: Ability to respond appropriately to challenges and unforeseen issues relating to change and ambiguity in the external environment
- Personal motivation skills: Demonstrated commitment to the organization and ability to set and diligently pursue high performance standards
- Occupational/technical skills: Knowledge and skills need to do the job and oversee the work of others including technical competence in relevant fields such as engineering
- Cognitive skills: Ability to analyze problems and reach decisions, financial and quantitative skills, innovativeness and resourcefulness, and skills at identifying and managing details

## Management Skills Training

Management educators have a keen interest in identifying the most "important" management skills so that they can make informed decisions about the curriculum for training both students about to enter the workplace and practicing managers looking to be more effective in their current positions and/or move up the ladder in the organizational hierarchy. It is generally agreed that managers at all levels need to have technical, human, conceptual, and design skills; however, managers at different levels in the organizational hierarchy need to be more proficient at some skills than with others and the operational function in which a manager is acting will obviously influence the skills and experience requirements he or she must satisfy. That said, human skills appear to be the most important for all managers, from the factory floor to the corner office executive suites, and thus it is not surprising that there has been a strong wave of advocacy for finding effective means for incorporating development of human skills into management training and education programs.

### Tasks and Skills of Effective Managers

An effective manager engages in various tasks and activities (e.g., planning, organizing, staffing, directing, coordinating, and controlling) to design and maintain an environment in which people can work together efficiently to achieve selected organizational goals and create a "surplus" for organizational stakeholders. In order successfully complete these tasks and activities managers must cultivate and master a number of important skills including the ability to develop and nurture peer relationships, negotiation and conflict resolution skills, the ability to motivate and inspire subordinates, establishment and maintenance of information networks, the ability to communicate effectively when disseminating information, and the ability to make decisions and allocate resources in conditions of extreme ambiguity.

Development of management training programs must be discussed in the broader context of debates regarding the efficacy of standard programs that have traditionally been offered at business and management schools. Many have argued that educational programs that simply pour in management principles that students play back on examinations are of little use since they fail to teach "how to manage."[33] In his legendary article written in the mid-1970s, Mintzberg offered the following critique:

---

[33] Latif, D. Winter 2002. "Model for Teaching the Management Skills Component of Managerial Effectiveness to Pharmacy Students." *American Journal of Pharmaceutical Education* 66, pp. 377–80, 378 (citing Whetten, D., and K. Cameron. 1983. "Management Skill Training: A Needed Addition to the Management Curriculum." *Organizational Behavior Teaching Journal* 8, no. 2, pp. 10–15; Mintzberg, H. 1975. "The Manager's Job: Folklore and Fact." *Harvard Business Review* 53, no. 4, pp. 49–71; Pfeffer, J. 1981. *Power in Organizations*, 22–78. Marshfield, MA: Pitman Publishing; and Porras, J., and B. Anderson. 1981. "Improving Managerial Effectiveness through Modeling-based Training." *Organizational Dynamics* 9, no. 4, pp. 60–77).

Management schools will begin the serious training of managers when skill training takes its place next to cognitive learning. Cognitive learning is detached and informational, like reading a book or listening to a lecture. No doubt much important cognitive material must be assimilated by the manager-to-be. But cognitive learning no more makes a manager than a swimmer. The latter will drown the first time he jumps into the water if his coach never takes him out of the lecture hall, gets him wet, and gives him feedback on his performance. Our management schools need to identify the skills managers use, select students who show potential in these skills, put the students into situations where these skills can be practiced, and then give them systematic feedback on their performance.[34]

There should be no doubt that management principles, the so-called "cognitive learning" that Mintzberg was referring to in the quote earlier, provide an important foundation for managers, including tools that can be deployed when practicing activities, such as "strategic planning," that rely on conceptual and design skills. Technical skills are also necessary to provide immediate and personal assistance to subordinates on issues they may be having with completing their assigned tasks and activities and in building credibility when managing function-based groups. However, there is clearly a gaping hole in the curriculum that needs to be filled, a step that is even more important given the critical nature of human skills to effective management, motivated, and satisfied workers and attainment of overall productivity.

In order to address this issue, the first step is achieving a consensus on just what skills are needed. The list compiled by Cameron and Whetten and presented earlier is a good starting point. Research conducted by Luthans et al. suggested that effective managers had significantly different and better skill levels with respect to building power and influence, communication with insiders and outsiders, goal setting, managing conflict,

---

[34] Mintzberg, H. 1975. "The Manager's Job: Folklore and Fact." *Harvard Business Review* 53, no. 4, pp. 49–71, 60.

and decision-making.[35] In addition, interpersonal skills, written communication, enthusiasm, technical competence, and the ability to listen and give counsel emerged as critical skills in another study of administrators.[36] Camp et al. took a different approach and identified the following major reasons why managers failed: ineffective communication skills, poor interpersonal skills, failure to clarify expectations, poor delegation, inability to develop teamwork, inability to motivate others and a lack of trust.[37] Finally, Latif reviewed what he characterized as a "representative sample of studies that relied on a heterogeneous mix of respondents from a multitude of diverse industries" to compile a list of the "most frequently cited managerial skills" that included verbal communication (including listening); managing time and stress; managing individual decisions; recognizing, defining and solving problems; motivating and influencing others; delegating; setting goals and articulating a vision; self-awareness; team building; and managing conflict.[38]

Latif noted that the most commonly identified characteristics of effective managers were all behavioral skills and were found to be relevant regardless of industry, the level of the manager in the organizational hierarchy or the job responsibilities of the manager.[39] Having identified what appears to be a reasonably acceptable pool of "skills," the question then

[35] Luthans, F., S. Rosenkrantz, and H. Hennessey. 1985. "What do Successful Managers Really Do?" An Observation Study of Managerial Activities." *Journal of Applied Behavioral Science* 21, no. 3, pp. 255–70.

[36] Curtis, D., J. Winsor, and D. Stephens. 1989. "National Preferences in Business and Communication Education." *Communication Education* 38, no. 1, pp. 6–15.

[37] Camp, R., M. Vielhaber, and J. Simonetti. 2001. *Strategic Interviewing: How to Hire Good People*, 5–76. San Francisco, CA: Jossey-Bass.

[38] Latif, D. Winter 2002. "Model for Teaching the Management Skills Component of Managerial Effectiveness to Pharmacy Students." *American Journal of Pharmaceutical Education* 66, no. 4, pp. 377–80, 379 (citing also discussions of other published management studies on the subject referred to in Whetten, D., and K. Cameron. 2002. *Developing Management Skills*, 3–297, 5th ed. Upper Saddle River, NJ: Prentice Hall).

[39] Id. at p. 379.

becomes how best to "teach" them. Latif explained some of the challenges in the following passage:

> Management skills are linked to a rather complex knowledge base (more so than other skills such as those associated with a trade or a sport). In additional, management skills are inexplicably connected to the interaction of other people. As such, effective use of these skills often involves a non-standardized approach to managing human beings (unlike a standardized approach to performing trade skills such as welding).[40]

Latif and others have suggested that effective "skills" training must include practical application (i.e., the opportunity to "practice," receive feedback, and apply the feedback in more practice opportunities); however, practice alone is not sufficient and students must also invest time and effort in gathering and understanding necessary "conceptual" knowledge.[41] Latif argued that the "most effective" approach to teaching and developing management skills is based on Social Learning Theory and calls for a teaching model that includes conceptual knowledge, observation of how others execute the particular skills and, finally, guided direct experience with feedback ("practice").[42] For example, new sales representatives might first go through a short orientation that exposes them to the requisite body of conceptual knowledge and then spend a week or two accompanying experienced sales representatives to observe how they do their jobs and apply the skills communicated during the orientation phase. Once the observation stage is over the new sales representatives would return to headquarters and "practice" applying the skills in workshops that include exercises, simulations, and role playing and where immediate feedback can be given by trainers.

---

[40] Id.

[41] Id. at p. 380.

[42] Id. (citing, as further resources relating to Social Learning Theory, Bandura, A. 1977. *A Social Learning Theory.* Upper Saddle River, NJ: Prentice Hall; and Kolb, D. 1984. *Experimental Learning: Experience as a Source of Learning and Development.* Upper Saddle River, NJ: Prentice Hall).

As noted earlier, Cameron and Whetten were interested in developing a model curriculum for "teaching management skills" and suggested a model that was, in fact, based on Social Learning Theory, albeit in what they referred to as a "modified form."[43] They began with a four step model that was widely used in management skill training initiatives and which included, in order, presentation of principles or behavioral guidelines derived from general theories of human behavior and empirical data on successful management practices, demonstration of the principles by the instructor using videos or written scripts, opportunities for practice relying on role playing and similar exercises and, finally, feedback on personal performance from the instructor and peers.[44] They then added two more features, preassessment and an application activity at the end of the process, to come with their own "suggested skill learning approach" with five components, each of which can be briefly explained as follows relying in large part on their own words[45]:

---

[43] Cameron, K., and D. Whetten. 1983. "A Model for Teaching Management Skills." *Organizational Behavior Teaching Journal* 8, no. 2, pp. 21–27, 23. According to Cameron and Whetten, additional and substantial support for the use and effectiveness of Social Learning Theory in management skills training can be found in Burnaska, R. 1976. "The Effects of Behavior Modeling Training upon Managers' Behavior and Employees' Perceptions." *Personnel Psychology* 29, no. 3, pp. 329–35; Latham, G., and L. Saari. 1979. "Application of Social-Learning Theory to Training Supervisors through Behavioral Modeling." *Journal of Applied Psychology* 64, no. 3, pp. 239–46; Moses, J., and R. Ritchie. 1976. "Supervisory Relationships Training: A Behavioral Evaluation of a Behavior Modeling Program." *Personnel Psychology* 29, no. 3, pp. 337–43; Porras, J., and B. Anderson. 1981. "Improving Managerial Effectiveness through Modeling-Based Training." *Organizational Dynamics* 9, no. 4, pp. 60–77; and Smith, P. 1976. "Management Modeling Training to Improve Morale and Customer Satisfaction." *Personnel Psychology* 29, no. 3, pp. 351–59.

[44] Cameron, K., and D. Whetten. 1983. "A Model for Teaching Management Skills." *Organizational Behavior Teaching Journal* 8, no. 2, pp. 21–27, 23 (citing Goldstein, A., and M. Sorcher. 1974. *Changing Supervisor Behavior*. New York, NY: Pergamon Internal Library).

[45] The description in the following paragraphs is adapted from the explanation presented by Cameron and Whetten in Cameron, K., and D. Whetten. 1983. "A Model for Teaching Management Skills." *Organizational Behavior Teaching Journal* 8, no. 2, pp. 21–27, 23–24.

- **_Skill Preassessment._** This step occurs at the beginning of each "skill learning experience" and focuses on assessing the current level of skill competence and knowledge in order to increase the efficiency of the learning process by identifying specific deficiencies in knowledge or performance that can then be addressed directly during the training. Common preassessment tools include questionnaires, surveys, questions about cases and role playing. Preassessment is necessary to provide students with their level of skill competency and provide them with motivation to improve by learning and applying the methods covered in the following steps.

- **_Skill Learning._** This second step involves presentation of conceptual material based on the most essential and relevant (i.e., "need-to-know" rather than "nice-to-know") theory and research in order to teach the correct principles and explain the rationale for the behavioral guidelines recommended during the training. Written texts are supplemented by lectures and discussions during which the instructors specify which behavioral guidelines are important, rather than relying on students to pry them out of theories, cases, and examples on their own. Proponents of this model emphasize that behavioral guidelines should be rigorously derived based on sound data and empirical testing rather than anecdotes and opinions so that students have a sound rationale for accepting and attempting to apply the principles.

- **_Skill Analysis._** The third step assesses understanding of the behavioral guidelines learned during the previous step through the analysis of case studies that include examples of appropriate and inappropriate skill performance. Students should be provided with opportunities to analyze how the behavioral principles are applicable to "real world" situations and problems. Case studies are one of the best ways to demonstrate skill analysis and can be presented in a number of formats including written cases, video tapes, audio recordings, and movies and students should be asked to critique the actions of managers depicted in the case studies in order to check their comprehension of the material and analyze a model of the skill being performed.

- **Skill Practice.** The fourth step shifts from observation to practicing the behavioral guidelines in a supportive atmosphere. Cameron and Whetten emphasize that students should "experiment" with the guidelines, rather than trying to mimic the style of a role model, and should be encouraged to adapt each set of behavioral principles to their particular personality and interpersonal style. Feedback should be provided not only from the instructor but also from peers, since this allows them to sharpen their own observation and perception skills and practice the important management skill of providing feedback to others. Feedback allows students to correct mistakes and experiment with alternative approaches. Skill practice activities include exercises, simulations, role playing, and group activities.

- **Skill Application.** The important final step of skill application focuses on transferring "classroom learning" to real-life situations, including actual practice accompanied by opportunities for feedback and continuing personal and professional development. Student are given specific assignments, both behavioral and written, to test how well they have learned the skill and how to apply it. Examples mentioned by Cameron and Whetten included teaching the skill to someone else, reporting on a personal effort to apply the principles in an appropriate setting, and confronting a problem in which performance of the skill is required. Instructors provide feedback on the assignments and assist students in their own self-analysis of their performance, thereby providing ongoing support for student efforts to refine and improve their performance.

Cameron and Whetten argued that their model had several important advantages over traditional teaching methods. For example, while their model relied on tried and true lecture and discussions techniques, it also incorporated personal diagnosis beginning with the pre-assessment stage and opportunities to practice the skills and obtain real-time feedback.

In addition, while use of case studies was not new, their value as a teaching tool was enhanced by the other steps included in the model, particularly the insistence on presentations of behavioral guidelines that would allow students to be more astute reviewers of the situations and problems embedded in the cases. Finally, they noted that the experimental exercises and group participation used in their curriculum went beyond mere observation to become valuable opportunities to actually practice the skills that were being taught and gather suggestions on how to improve performance. Cameron and Whetten did concede that implementation of their model would require overcoming a variety of challenging issues, particularly the need for smaller class sizes and additional time during those classes to properly and effectively carry out each of the steps in the suggested model. They also noted that faculty members would themselves need to develop the skills that they are attempting to teach and model for their students and that faculty members would need to embrace "skill training" as a key activity even though it may reduce the time they might otherwise have available to devote to research activities that are important to their own careers.[46]

In order for their skills training to be effective and properly focused, managers must have some means to assess how they are doing. Mintzberg was clear in his belief that the managerial position was extremely complex and urged managers to take the time to be "introspective about their work" by reviewing and answering a lengthy list of 14 sets of "self-study questions."[47] The following list of the initial questions from each set provides an insight into the type of assessment that Mintzberg recommended:

- Where do I get my information, and how?
- What information do I disseminate?

---

[46] Id. at p. 24. For a detailed discussion of their model and examples of teaching tools, see Whetten, D., and K. Cameron. 2002. *Developing Management Skills*, 5th ed. Upper Saddle River, NJ: Prentice Hall.

[47] Mintzberg, H. March/April 1990. "The Manager's Job: Folklore and Fact." *Harvard Business Review*, 163–76. For further discussion of Mintzberg's views on managerial roles, see "Management Roles and Activities" prepared and distributed by the Sustainable Entrepreneurship Project (www.seproject.org).

- Do I tend to act before information is in?
- What pace of change am I asking my organization to tolerate?
- Am I sufficiently well-informed to pass judgment on subordinate's proposals?
- What is my vision for this organization?
- How do my subordinates react to my managerial style?
- What kind of external relationships do I maintain, and how?
- Is there any system to my time scheduling, or am I just reacting to the pressures of the moment?
- Do I overwork?
- Am I too superficial in what I do?
- Do I spend too much time on current, tangible activities?
- Do I use the different media appropriately?
- How did I blend my personal rights and duties?

Each of the initial questions was supported by ideas for additional assessment. For example, the last question regarding blending of personal rights and duties was accompanied by suggestions that managers analyze whether their obligations consumed all their time and create opportunities to free themselves from some of those obligations so that they are able to focus on softer, yet quite important, topics such as their unique role as the organizational "entrepreneur." The meaning of each of the questions obviously evolves over time. Consider that the question regarding appropriate use of different media was first posed in 1990, well before e-mail and the other social media tools that predominate today were introduced and widely available. At that time, Mintzberg emphasized the amount and quality of face-to-face communications engaged in by managers, including participation in meetings. The situation has changed significantly since then and managers now face new challenges in sifting through the flood of information that is now available and incorporate new technological tools into their roles as "liaison," "disseminator," and "spokesperson."

### Simple Assessment Tools for Managers

The list of Mintzberg's self-study questions in the text includes only the initial question in the set of questions that he created for each of the

14 topics and reference should be made to the full list of a better understanding of the issues that he observed in a particular topical area. For example, a manager concerned about how well he or she is carrying out the informational role associated with the managerial position should carefully consider the following questions:

- Where do I get my information and how?
- Can I make greater use of my contacts?
- Can other people do some of my scanning?
- In what areas is my knowledge weakest, and how can I get others to provide me with the information I need?
- Do I have sufficiently powerful mental models of those things I must understand within the organization and in its environment?
- What information do I disseminate?
- How important is that information to my subordinates?
- Do I keep too much information to myself because disseminating it is time consuming or inconvenient?
- How can I get more information to others so they can make better decisions?
- Do I tend to act before information is in or do I wait so long for all the information that opportunities pass me by?

Mintzberg's questions are just one of many tools that managers can use to assess their skills. Online tests are available to provide insights into what type of management style a manager is likely to demonstrate to his or her subordinates and Griffin has created a library of questionnaires for use in assessing management skills in a number of areas including self-awareness, beliefs and values, goal setting, enhancing motivation, managing diversity, mental abilities, and using and managing teams. For example, Griffin's assessment of "skills of effective managers" asks respondents to consider how they see themselves with respect to the following statements:

- I am at ease in written and oral communication including listening

- I handle stress well and seldom have time management problems
- I have no trouble making decisions that affect me and/or others
- I can identify, analyze, and solve problems effectively
- I am effective at getting others to perform at high levels
- I delegate tasks to others to help them learn and to involve them in the activity at hand
- I set goals and establish a long-term vision for everything I do and can help others do the same
- I am keenly aware of my own strengths and weaknesses
- I work well with groups and can help others develop into effective teams
- I handle conflict well and am able to help others resolve their difference

While this type of assessment obviously does not delve into details it nonetheless can be used by managers to identify roles and skills they may have neglected and such information can be used for development of training and self-improvement plans.

*Sources*: Mintzberg, H. March/April 1990. "The Manager's Job: Folklore and Fact." *Harvard Business Review*, pp. 163–76; Griffin, R. 2002. *Fundamentals of Management*, 3rd ed. Independence, KY: Cengage Learning. http://college.cengage.com/business/griffin/fundamentals/3e/students/ assessment/; "What is Your Management Style," http://quotev.com/ quiz/481888/What-Is-Your-Management-Style/; and "Test Your Management Style with this 6 Point Quiz," http://training-course.org/man-agement-style-6-point-quiz.php

# CHAPTER 3

# Management Styles

## Introduction

As with other topics that have been intensely reviewed in the management literature, there is a wide array of definitions of the term "management style." A fairly simple approach is to view management style simply as the way that an organization is managed.[1] Schleh referred to management style as "… [t]he adhesive that binds diverse operations and functions together. It is the philosophy or set of principles by which you capitalize on the abilities of your people. It is not a procedure on 'how to do,' but is the management framework for doing. A management style is a way of life operating throughout the enterprise. It permits an executive to rely on the initiative of his people."[2] Yu and Yeh defined management style as "a preferred way of managing people in order to bind diverse operations and functions together, as well as to exercise control over employees, and is considered as a set of practices that has been adopted either by an individual, a department, or whole organization."[3] Others have

---

[1] Quang, T., and N. Vuong. 2002. "Management Styles and Organisational Effectiveness in Vietnam." *Research and Practice in Human Resource Management* 10, no. 2, pp. 36–55.

[2] Schleh, E. August 1977. "A Matter of Management Style." *Management Review,* pp. 9–13, 10.

[3] Yu, P.L., and Q.J. Yeh. 2018. "Asian and Western Management Styles, Innovative Culture and Professionals' Skills." http://scribd.com/doc/61439046/HR-Abstracts (accessed December 17, 2018) (citing Schleh, C. 1977. "A Matter of Management Style." *Management Review* 66, pp. 9–13; Clear, F., and K. Dickson. 2005. "Teleworking Practice in Small and Medium-Sized Firms: Management Style and Worker Autonomy." *New Technology Work and Employment* 20, pp. 220–33; and Morris, T., and M. Pavett. 1992. "Management Style and Productivity in Two Cultures." *Journal of International Business Studies* 23, pp. 169–79).

approached descriptions of management style by attempting to identify various functions of the manager. For example, Quang and Vuong noted that Khandwalla defined management style as "the distinctive way in which an organisation makes decisions and discharges various functions, including goal setting, formulation and implementation of strategy, all basic management activities, corporate image building and dealing with key stakeholders."[4]

Quang and Vuong pointed out that there is no single management style that applies in all instances and that an organization's "operating conditions" will influence the style that is selected.[5] This assertion is consistent with other indications that management styles are influenced and determined by a number of different factors. Some believe that societal culture has the biggest impact on the management styles selected and used by organizations operating within a society and there is ample evidence for the proposition that one can find distinctive management styles in different countries such as France, India, Japan, the United States, and Vietnam.[6] This has led to the argument that each societal culture has its own "core style" of management based on the values and norms that predominate in that culture, with some allowances for local variations.[7] However, other researchers have conducted exhaustive studies of large number of organizations in the same country and found evidence of a wide range of management styles within the same societal culture. For example, Burns and Stalker identified two very different management styles in the United Kingdom—organic and mechanistic[8]—and Khandwalla was able to come up with seven categories of management style in

---

[4] Quang, T., and N. Vuong. 2002. "Management Styles and Organisational Effectiveness in Vietnam." *Research and Practice in Human Resource Management* 10, no. 2, pp. 36–55 (citing Khandwalla, P. 1995. *Management Styles*. New Delhi: Tata McGraw-Hill Publishing Co. Ltd).

[5] Id.

[6] For further discussion, see "Comparative Management Studies" prepared and distributed by the Sustainable Entrepreneurship Project (www.seproject.org).

[7] Evans, W., K. Han, and D. Sculli. 1989. "A Cross-cultural Comparison of Managerial Styles." *Journal of Management Development* 8, no. 3, pp. 5–13.

[8] Burns, T., and G. Stalker. 1961. *The Management of Innovation*. London: Tavistock.

Canada[9] and found variations in management styles between firms in different industries in India as well as differences among Indian firms operating in the same industry.[10]

While not making it any easier to create prescriptions for effective management styles, the reality seems to be that there are a number of factors that likely have an impact on the selection and effectiveness of management styles, including the type of organization, business purpose and activities of the organization, size of the organization, operating environment, corporate culture, societal culture, information technology and communication and, finally, the personal style and behavior of the owner or chief executive. Quang and Vuong noted that the authoritarian management styles often used in state-owned enterprises in many developing countries reflected the governing styles of their political leaders.[11] They also suggested that in small and mid-sized firms it could be expected that the size of the organization would lead to the personal style of the owner or chief executive having a significant impact on how the firm operated and subordinates behaved.[12] Lewis argued that advances in communications and information processing technology could change the way that managers work and interact with their subordinates.[13] Reddin's model of management styles emphasized the importance of "situational factors" and was based on the fundamental principle that managerial behaviors and styles will and must vary depending on where the manager is in the organizational hierarchy and the type of activities that he or she is overseeing.[14] Finally, management styles will change as firms transition to new

---

[9] Khandwalla, P. 1977. *The Design of Organization*. New York, NY: Harcourt Brace Jovanovich.

[10] Khandwalla, P. 1980. "Management in Our Backyard." *Vikalpa* 5, pp. 173–84.

[11] Quang, T., and N. Vuong. 2002. "Management Styles and Organisational Effectiveness in Vietnam." *Research and Practice in Human Resource Management* 10, no. 2, pp. 36–55.

[12] Id. (citing Davidmann, M. 1995. *Style of Management and Leadership*, 2nd ed.).

[13] Lewis, P., S. Goodman, and P. Fandt. 2001. *Management: Challenges in the 21st Century*, 3rd ed. Mason, OH: South Western College Publishing.

[14] Reddin, W. April 1967. "The 3-D Management Style Theory: A Typology Based On Task and Relationships Orientation." *Training and Development Journal*, pp. 8–17.

business models based on changing trends in the marketplace, such as greater emphasis on quality and customer service and satisfaction.[15]

Quang and Vuong provided a useful short summary of some of the ideas regarding "formal" management styles that have been developed and described by scholars over the past few decades[16]:

The often cited distinction between "organic" and "mechanistic" management styles was first introduced by Burns and Stalker.[17]

Japanese management style attracted the attention of a number of scholars in the 1980s and has been said to feature an emphasis on "paternalism, lifetime employment, seniority, lifelong learning, collective decision making, hard work, cooperation ethics, continuous adaptation and improvement."[18]

Khandwalla studied companies in the United States, Canada, and India and concluded that there were five fundamental dimensions that served as the foundation of the styles selected and used by managers: risk taking, technocracy, flexibility, participation, and authoritarianism.[19]

Peters and Waterman responded to the interest in Japanese management styles by identifying the contrasting element of American management style, which they said included more emphasis on core values, highly flexible structures, business unit autonomy, interactivity, and innovation.[20]

---

[15] Dolan, S., and S. Garcia. 2002. "Managing by Values: Cultural Redesign for Strategic Organizational Change at the Dawn of the Twenty-First Century." *Journal of Management Development* 21, no. 2, pp. 101–17.

[16] Quang, T., and N. Vuong. 2002. "Management Styles and Organisational Effectiveness in Vietnam." *Research and Practice in Human Resource Management* 10, no. 2, pp. 36–55.

[17] Burns, T., and G. Stalker. 1961. *The Management of Innovation.* London: Tavistock.

[18] Pascale, T., and A. Athos. 1983. *The Arts of Japanese Management.* New York, NY: Simon and Schuster; and Wilkins, A., and W. Ouchi. 1983. "Efficient Culture: Exploring the Relationship Between Culture and Organizational Performance." *Administrative Science Quarterly* 28, pp. 465–81.

[19] Khandwalla, P. 1995. *Management Styles.* New Delhi: Tata McGraw-Hill Publishing Co. Ltd.; and Khandwalla, P. 1995. "Effectiveness Management Styles: An Indian Study." *Journal of Euro-Asian Management* 1, no. 1, pp. 39–64.

[20] Peters, T., and R. Waterman., Jr. 1982. *In Search of Excellence.* New York, NY: Harper & Row.

Management styles are widely studied because research indicates that they are significant factor in determining overall organizational effectiveness. It is obvious that the elements of management style have a direct influence on how individual employees and work groups perform their operational activities, including the actual sequence of tasks, the goals they are pursuing, and how they feel about their roles within the organization. Management style also determines the level of cooperation within the organization and how people within the organization interrelate with one another and with customers, suppliers, and other stakeholders outside of the organization.[21] Measuring "organizational effectiveness" is not always an easy proposition; however, in their study of Vietnamese management styles Quang and Vuong suggested that indicators of effectiveness might include employee satisfaction, profitability, growth rate, competitiveness, financial strength, public image and goodwill, and technological leadership.[22]

## Dimensions of Management Styles

In order to facilitate the efficient and productive comparative study of management styles researchers have created models using various managerial practices or activities as dimensions which can be used to organize data and define the characteristics of particular styles and differentiate them from others. One can see both consensus and divergence among the dimensions that have been selected by researchers; however, one lesson seems to be that clarity of analysis and understanding likely demands that the number of dimensions be kept to a manageable number in order to provide meaningful guidance to managers with respect to areas that they need to focus on as they interact with subordinates and carry out their day-to-day activities.

---

[21] Quang, T., and N. Vuong. 2002. "Management Styles and Organisational Effectiveness in Vietnam." *Research and Practice in Human Resource Management* 10, no. 2, pp. 36–55 (citing Davidmann, M. 1995. *Style of Management and Leadership*, 2nd ed.).

[22] Id. For further discussion of organizational performance, see "Organizational Performance and Effectiveness" prepared and distributed by the Sustainable Entrepreneurship Project (www.seproject.org).

Many of the proposed models have been based on just two dimensions which have been used to generate four distinctive management styles based on different combinations of scores or placement on the two dimensions. For example, a well-known model that used assertiveness and cooperativeness as the two dimensions for analysis suggested the following possible management styles: "avoiding" (low assertiveness and low cooperativeness); "accommodating" (low assertiveness and high cooperativeness); "competing" (high assertiveness and low cooperativeness); "collaborating" (high assertiveness and high cooperativeness); and "compromising" (mid-level on both assertiveness and cooperativeness).[23] In this model "assertiveness" focused on managerial behaviors that were focused inward while "cooperativeness" focused on managerial behaviors directed at subordinates. An assertive manager tends to be confrontational while an unassertive manager is avoidant and the degree of cooperativeness is directly related to how reasonable a manager is in his or her dealings and communications with subordinates. Another often cited two-dimensional model focused on how roles and responsibilities were designed and used the dimensions of "programmability" and "capability for autonomy."[24] This model generated three types of managerial styles: "autocratic/benevolent autocratic" (high programmability/low job autonomy); "consultative/participative" (low programmability/low job autonomy and high programmability/high job autonomy); and "consensus/laissez-faire" (low programmability/high job autonomy). Other two-dimensional sets have included "concern for personal goals" and "concern for relationships," and "concern for people" (relationships) and "concern for results" (tasks or performance).[25]

---

[23] The assertiveness/cooperativeness model was first popularized by Thomas and Kilmann, who developed the Thomas-Kilmann Conflict Mode Instrument to understand how different conflict-handling styles influenced personal and group dynamics and assist managers in selecting the most appropriate style for a specific situation.

[24] Flamholtz, E., and Y. Randle. 2007. *Growing Pains: Transitioning From an Entrepreneurship to a Professionally Managed Firm*, 4th ed.

[25] See, for example, Eckstein, D. October 1997. "Styles of Conflict Management." *Family Journal* 5, no. 4, pp. 240–44; Blake, R., and J. Mouton. 1964. *The Managerial Grid: The Key to Leadership Excellence*; and Reddin, W. April 1967.

While two-dimensional models are relatively easy to grasp, other researchers have argued for integrating more than just two factors into the process of developing a profile of managerial style. Quang and Vuong proposed a model of a "management system" that included the following items or dimensions: leadership style, degree of decentralization/delegation, communication pattern, quality controls, authority definition, trust, and confidence in subordinates, planning term, personnel policy, control devices, training programs, motivation, employee morale, absenteeism, and productivity.[26] With respect to each item or dimension Quang and Vuong also provided specific characteristics for each item or dimension which could be used as a basis of comparison between organizations or enterprise sectors. For example, when Quang and Vuong examined "leadership style" they focused on characteristics such as how much attention the supervisor paid to employees' interests and opinions, close supervision, encouragement of work teams, the amount of direction given from the top, the amount of freedom given to subordinates and the extent to which the supervisor delegated authority to subordinates. When "decision making" was being analyzed Quang and Vuong measured the degree of employees' participation in decision making, the degree of contribution of functional departments in decision making, the use of new methods and technologies in decision making, and the level of support from employees for decisions made by top management.

Quang and Vuong used their model to analyze and compare the characteristics of the management systems used in the state, private, and joint venture sectors in Vietnam and concluded that "there was no single management style that cut across all the three types of enterprises."[27] In the state sector, for example, it was not surprising given the heritage

---

"The 3-D Management Style Theory: A Typology Based On Task and Relationships Orientation." *Training and Development Journal*, pp. 8–17.

[26] Quang, T., and N. Vuong. 2002. "Management Styles and Organisational Effectiveness in Vietnam." *Research and Practice in Human Resource Management* 10, no. 2, pp. 36–55.

[27] For detailed discussion of the findings of Quang and Vuong with respect to Vietnamese business organizations, see "Comparative Management Studies" prepared and distributed by the Sustainable Entrepreneurship Project (www.seproject.org).

of centralized planning that the most prevalent managerial styles were bureaucratic, familial, conservative, and authoritarian styles and that common management practices included "clear reporting relationships, formal communication and strict control." In the private sector, however, the predominance of family-owned businesses explained the popularity of the familial management style with the owner treating the workers as part of one large family. As for management practices among these types of businesses, the researcher found a preference for tight controls and coordination overseen by managers who were relatives of the owner. Finally, firms in the joint venture sector, which necessarily was subject to the influence of foreign partners and their preference for so-called "modern principles of management," were more likely than firms in the other sectors to embrace elements of the participative management style.

Bloom and Van Reenen analyzed 18 basic management practices or dimensions; however, when presenting their findings they focused on three discernable groups of dimensions which they identified as "monitoring," "targets," and "incentives." The dimensions selected by Culpan and Kucukemiroglu for their comparative study of management styles in the United States and Japan included supervisory style, decision making, communication, control, interdepartmental relations, and paternalistic orientation.[28] Comparative research conducted by Weihrich and Yu and Yeh was based on dimensions that included planning, organizing, staffing, leading and controlling, decision making, leadership, communication, goals, motivation, and power distance.[29] Other scholars have attempted to match management styles to organizational values/culture,

---

[28] Culpan, R., and O. Kucukemiroglu. 1993. "A Comparison of US and Japanese Management Styles and Unit Effectiveness." *Management International Review* 33, pp. 27–42. For a review of the results of their comparison of US and Japanese management styles, see "Comparative Management Studies" prepared and distributed by the Sustainable Entrepreneurship Project (www.seproject.org).

[29] See Weihrich, H. March/April 1990. "Management Practices in the United States, Japan and the People's Republic of China." *Industrial Management*, pp. 3–7; and Yu, P.L., and Q.J. Yeh. 2012. "Asian and Western Management Styles, Innovative Culture and Professionals' Skills." http://scribd.com/doc/61439046/HR-Abstracts (accessed January 29, 2012). For discussion of each of these studies, see "Comparative Management Studies" prepared and distributed by the Sustainable Entrepreneurship Project (www.seproject.org).

environmental factors (e.g., turbulence, diversity, restrictiveness, and technological complexity), and factors personal to the manager such as his or her instrumental values, underlying emotional intelligence capabilities, or level of maturity.

## Khandwalla's Categories of Management Styles

While many researchers constructed their ideas regarding management styles on data collected among US-based organizations, Khandwalla relied on an empirical study of 90 organizations in India to define 10 categories of "management styles"—conservative, entrepreneurial, professional, bureaucratic, organic, authoritarian, participative, intuitive, familial, and altruistic—with the following key features[30]:

- Conservative: Bias for preserving and extending whatever has worked, cautious in innovating and/or changing status quo, predisposed to pursuit of diversification and growth in familiar directions, reliant on traditions that preserve the strengths of the past and generally conservative personality traits but not necessarily
- Entrepreneurial: Indulges in calculated risk taking, pioneering, innovation, and rapid growth
- Professional: Adapts scientific optimization-oriented approach to management, uses sophisticated management tools and techniques, and undertakes long range planning
- Bureaucratic: Emphasis on orderly management, accountability, and formalization of rules, regulations, and procedures
- Organic: Deep commitment to flexibility, innovation, responsiveness to change, teamwork and interactive, feedback-based decision making
- Authoritarian: Emphasis on discipline and obedience
- Participative: Committed to an ideology of collective, consensus-based decision making

---

[30] Khandwalla, P. 1995. "Effectiveness Management Styles: An Indian Study." *Journal of Euro-Asian Management* 1, no. 1, pp. 39–64, 43–46.

- Intuitive: Shows faith in experience, common sense, and intuitive judgment based on good rules of thumb or heuristics learned from experience
- Familial: Anchored in the notion that to achieve organizational cohesiveness and loyalty of employees to the organization the organization must treat its employees like family members and look after their needs
- Altruistic: Belief that the organization is an instrumentality of some larger social good and not just a vehicle for profit maximization

Khandwalla noted that several of the management styles have been identified as especially useful in particular situations and environments. For example, an entrepreneurial approach is necessary for efforts of developing countries to diversify their industrial base and pursue rapid growth of outputs. A professional approach works well for managing new and complicated technology-intensive industries in a complex global environment. An organic approach is often recommended for organizations operating in fast changing environments. The bureaucratic management style has been well documented and often associated with larger organizations, particularly those in the public sector, that are presumed to require processes that ensure accountability, equity, orderliness, and operating efficiency. The authoritarian management style was often used in developing countries during their colonial periods as a means for dealing with the perception that the local work ethic was weak and the task environment was hostile. The polar opposite of authoritarianism, the participative style, focuses on fostering motivation and cooperation and is useful in situation where managers value diverse perspectives and input before decisions are made and executed. Finally, the altruistic style was thought to be useful in developing countries launching major social projects, such as initiatives to alleviate poverty, improve infrastructure, or bolster the local education system.

## Thornton's "Big 3" Management Styles

Thornton argued that there are three basic management styles—directing ("tell employees what to do"), discussing ("ask questions and listen"), and delegating ("let employees figure it out on their own")—and that the characteristics of each of these styles can be explained using dimensions such as communication strategies, goal-setting, and decision-making procedures, performance monitoring procedures and the methods used for rewarding and recognizing the work of subordinates.[31] Thornton counseled that managers should be adept at each of the styles and must be able to diagnose the situation before deciding what management style to use. He also observed that management style is an evolutionary process and that as employees gain experience, skills, and confidence the manager should become more comfortable with granting employees more freedom and transitioning his or her preferred management style from directing to discussing and, finally, to delegating.[32]

The "directing" style places major control squarely in the hands of the manager, who assumes full responsibility for assigning duties and roles among subordinates, setting standards, and defining goals and expectations. This style is appropriate when specific orders need to be given in order to complete specific and well-defined tasks. When the directing style is used communication generally takes the form of specific directions from management, short term goals are set by management with little or no input from subordinates, formal control systems are used to monitor performance, and rewards are distributed based on how well subordinates follow and carry out the orders issued by management.

A manager using the "discussing" style makes an effort to discuss relevant issues with subordinates and creates an environment in which communication flows more smoothly and both managers and employees feel free and empowered to present ideas, ask questions, provide feedback, and coaching and challenge assumptions. Managers using this style have developed the capacity to listen to the concerns of their followers and

---

[31] The discussion in this section is adapted from Thornton, P. 2008. *The Big 3 Management Styles*. Oshawa, Ontario: Multi-Media Publications. Thornton has also written about leadership styles and skills and promoted the idea that leaders should provide challenge, coaching and confidence to their followers in order to provide the highest value to their organizations. See, for example, Thornton, P. 2001. *Be the Leader, Make the Difference*, 2nd ed. Santa Ana, CA: Griffin Publishing Group.

[32] Id.

facilitate meetings at which issues relating to work activities are discussed and debated. The discussing style gets people involved in the process of setting goals and making decisions and builds greater commitment among subordinates with respect to the goals of the units because they had a hand in setting them. Performance is monitored by managers and subordinates and the criteria for rewards and recognition is expanded to include the quality of contributions made to discussions, social skills, and openness in sharing information and opinions with the group.

Finally, the "delegating" style features a high level of autonomy for subordinates as managers set general expectations yet transfer substantial responsibility for the details of meeting those expectations to subordinates. Not surprisingly, it is recommended that this approach be limited to situations where the subordinates have a substantial amount of training and experience and thus are capable of acting without much direct supervision. Communication within groups using the delegating style varies depending on the situation and can either "one way" or "two way." Goals may be set by the manager alone or by the manager in collaboration with representatives from the subordinate group; however, regardless of how goals are established the hallmark of this type of style is the subordinates are given the independence and autonomy to decide on their own about the best way to pursue and achieve those goals. Since managers are not involved in the details of the design of specific tasks and activities, they do require continuous and timely feedback on performance to ensure that satisfactory progress is being made toward completion of the agreed goals. Rewards and recognition when the delegating style is used are based on efficiency and the ability of subordinates to perform well when asked to work autonomously.

## Reddin's 3-D Management Style Theory

A number of scholars and researchers have observed that the psychological managerial typologies created by many leading management theorists are actually all based on two underlying variables—task orientation and relationships orientation.[33] For example, the model of managerial types

---

[33] Reddin, W. April 1967. "The 3-D Management Style Theory: A Typology Based On Task and Relationships Orientation." *Training and Development Journal*, pp. 8–17.

proposed by Blake and Mouton in their "Managerial Grid" contrasts managers that have a concern for production (i.e., a task orientation) with managers that are more concerned with "people" (i.e., a relationships orientation).[34] Similarly, McGregor's "Theory X" is arguably task oriented while his "Theory Y" is more relationships oriented.[35] Carron focused on "initiating structure" (i.e., a task orientation) and "consideration" (i.e., a relationships orientation) as tools for describing management behavior that allowed for identification of four managerial styles: laissez-faire, democratic, autocratic, and paternalistic.[36]

Following review of the orientations and definitions used in, and the findings of, various studies, Reddin suggested definitions of both task and relationships orientation. With regard to task orientation, he defined it as "the extent to which a manager is likely to direct his own and his subordinates' efforts toward goal attainment ... [t]hose with high task orientation tend to direct more than others through planning, communicating, informing, scheduling and introducing new ideas." Relationships orientation was defined as "the extent to which a manager is likely to have highly personal job relationships characterized by mutual trust, respect for subordinates' ideas and consideration of their feelings ... [t]hose with high relationships orientation have good rapport with others and good two-way communication."[37]

Reddin went on to suggest that managerial styles can be categorized and defined by the four possible ways that managers emphasize tasks and/or relationships and developed the following four-type typology of "Latent Non-Normative" styles: "separated," which is the situation where a manager appears to act without concern for either tasks or relationships; "relationships," which is the situation where a manager clearly emphasizes

---

[34] Blake, R., and J. Mouton. 1964. *The Managerial Grid*. Houston, TX: Gulf Publishing.

[35] McGregor, D. 1960. *The Human Side of Enterprise*. New York, NY: McGraw-Hill.

[36] Carron, T. 1964. "Human Relations Training and Attitude Change: A Vector Analysis." *Personnel Psychology* 17, no. 4, pp. 403–24.

[37] Reddin, W. April 1967. "The 3-D Management Style Theory: A Typology Based On Task and Relationships Orientation." *Training and Development Journal* 21, no. 4, pp. 8–17.

concerns about relationships over tasks (i.e., relationship oriented); "task," which is the opposite of "relationships" and is present when managers focus primarily on tasks (i.e., task oriented); and "integrated," which is the situation where a manager attempts to be both task- and relationship-oriented. Reddin took pains to emphasize that "[n]o claims can be made that any one of these four styles is more effective than the other" and the managerial behavior required for successful performance will vary depending upon the particular situation. He noted, for example, that "[s]ome jobs, to be performed effectively, demand a high relationships orientation and low task orientation ... [s]ome require the opposite."[38]

Reddin argued that if the effectiveness of a particular style varied depending on the situation, then it was possible to create a model of eight managerial styles that included two behavioral counterparts, one that was less effective and one that was more effective, for each of his four Latent Non-Normative styles: for "separated" the less effective style was called "deserter" and the more effective style was called "bureaucratic"; for "relationships" the less effective style was called "missionary" and the more effective style was called "developer"; for "task" the less effective style was called "autocrat" and the more effective style was called "benevolent autocrat"; and for "integrated" the less effective style was called "compromiser" and the most effective style was called "executive." Reddin also supplied the following summary descriptions of each of the eight styles included in his "3-D" model[39]:

> **Deserter:** Managers using this style often display a lack of interest in both tasks and relationships (i.e., the "separated" Latent Non-Normative style) and are ineffective both because of this lack of

---

[38] Id. Reddin referred to the work of Strong, E.K., Jr. which appeared to support the proposition that "ideal" managerial behavior traits varied depending on the position and associated tasks and activities (i.e., differences could be identified between executives, production managers, sales managers, personnel managers, and other types of managers). See Strong, E.K., Jr. 1927. "Vocational Guidance of Executive." *Journal of Applied Psychology* 11, no. 5, pp. 331–47.

[39] Reddin, W. April 1967. "The 3-D Management Style Theory: A Typology Based On Task and Relationships Orientation." *Training and Development Journal* 21, no. 4, pp. 8–17.

interest and the impact of this style on the overall morale of subordinates. In addition to deserting, this type of manager may hinder performance in other ways by valueless intervention in work activities and/or by withholding necessary information.

*Bureaucrat:* Like deserters, bureaucrats are not really that interested in either task or relationship orientations and focus their efforts primarily on understanding and applying the rules and procedures that have been laid down for production. In contrast to the autocratic described below, the bureaucrat is effective because he or she does not disrupt morale by obvious disdain for tasks and relationships and follows the rules while maintaining a mask of interest.

*Missionary:* Managers using the missionary style place the highest value on harmony and relationships (i.e., the "relationships" Latent Non-Normative style); however, they are ineffective because they want so hard to be seen by themselves and others as a "good person" that they are unable to risk upsetting relationships in order to make decisions that are necessary for efficient production.

*Developer:* The developer style is the more effective of the two "relationships" Latent Non-Normative style, contrasting with the missionary style described earlier. Managers using this style place their implicit trust in those that work with them and see their roles as being primarily concerned with developing the talents of others and providing an overall working environment that is conducive to motivation and maximization of individual satisfaction. This approach can be highly effective in certain instances since it promotes a working environment in which everyone is committed to their personal development and to completion of their work. The risk of this style is that there may be times when the manager's high relationships orientation causes him or her to make decisions that put the personal development of subordinates ahead of the interests of the entire organization with respect to maximizing short- or long-term production and/or the development of subordinates who can succeed to the position occupied by the manager.

*Autocrat:* Autocrats are most interested in completing the immediate task above all other considerations, including relationships (i.e., the "tasks" Latent Non-Normative style). This lack of concern for relationships makes the autocratic style ineffective since subordinates act only out of fear and their dislike of the manager stifles their motivation and causes them to work only when direct pressure is applied by the manager.

*Benevolent Autocrat:* Benevolent autocrats place implicit trust in themselves and are concerned with completing both immediate and long-term tasks. In contrast to his or her ineffective counterpart, the "autocrat," the benevolent autocratic is effective because he or she has the skill and patience to induce subordinates to carry out his or her directives without creating resentment or reducing morale, either of which can undermine his or her ability to achieve the desired production goals.

*Compromiser:* Managers using the compromiser style recognize the advantages of both task and relationship orientations (i.e., the "integrated" Latent Non-Normative style); however, they are ineffective due to their inability to make sound decisions. Ambivalence is the term that is used to describe the manner in which compromisers act and decisions are generally made based on the most recent or heaviest pressure. This leads to a style focusing on minimizing immediate problems rather than taking the steps that may be needed to maximize long-term production. The compromiser is particularly interested in staying on the good side of those people whom he or she believes can have the largest influence on his or her career.

*Executive:* A manager using the executive style sees his or her job as maximizing the efforts of his or her subordinates with respect to both short- and long-term tasks. The executive is committed to both task and relationship orientations (i.e., the "integrated" Latent Non-Normative style) and this is evident to everyone in the organization. The executive seeks to act as a powerful motivator, sets high standards for production and performance, and is willing and able to treat subordinates differently in order to obtain results and create personal satisfaction for as many people as possible within the organization. The executive's ability to obtain results from both task and relationship orientations makes him or her extremely effective.

While Reddin referred to the eight styles as "more" or "less" effective he counseled that the proper focus should be on "style demands of the situation" that the manager is in.[40] The "demands" are a function of the style demands of the job; the style demands of the superior, which are derived from the corporate philosophy and the superior's own preferred style; and the style demands of the subordinates, which are derived from the their expectations and their own styles. Reddin noted, for example, that in jobs where an orientation to routine was necessary the "separated" style of "bureaucracy" might be most effective; however, if the separated style was used in an aggressive sales organization it would likely take the form of the "deserter."[41]

## National Management Styles

At a basic level a manager's style refers to the characteristic ways in which he or she makes decisions regarding the group that he or she oversees and the methods that he or she uses when relating to his or her subordinates within that group. Managers have a wide array of functions and responsibilities—planning, organizing, staffing, leading, controlling, motivating, and decision making—and the manner in which they discharge those functions depends on a variety of factors, one of which is almost certainly the societal culture in which the manager and his or her subordinates are operating.[42] While many have argued that the increasing rate of globalization in the business arena is causing convergence among management styles that is overriding cultural differences, researchers continue to explore the characteristics of specific national management styles.[43] Some studies focus specifically on one country, a process referred to by anthropologists as ethnography and which includes in-depth analysis and description of

---

[40] Id. at p. 15.

[41] Id. at pp. 15 and 16.

[42] For discussion of the various managerial functions and responsibilities, see "Management Roles and Activities" prepared and distributed by the Sustainable Entrepreneurship Project (www.seproject.org).

[43] Information on management styles and practices in various countries is available in the Regional and Countries Studies materials prepared and distributed by the Sustainable Entrepreneurship Project (www.seproject.org).

the customary social behaviors of a single identifiable group of people using techniques such as participant observation; however, a good deal of what appears in more recent assessments of national management styles is based on the practice of ethnology, which is the comparative study of two or more cultures that looks at a narrower set of data related to a particular topic and seeks to compare and contrast the various cultures.

There are several different models of management style that may be used for descriptive and comparative purposes. One method for modeling a manager's style and practices focuses on a small set of specific characteristics and activities such as supervisory style, decision making style and processes, communication patterns, control mechanisms, management of interdepartmental relationships and, finally, the strength of paternalistic orientation when interacting with subordinates.[44] Another method of describing "management styles" which may be particularly useful when studying developing countries is the model created by Khandwalla after studying 90 organizations in India, research that caused him to recognize and describe 10 categories of management styles: conservative, entrepreneurial, professional, bureaucratic, organic, authoritarian, participative, intuitive, familial, and altruistic.[45]

---

[44] Culpan, R., and O. Kucukemiroglu. 1993. "A Comparison of US and Japanese Management Styles and Unit Effectiveness." *Management International Review*, pp. 27–42.

[45] Khandwalla, P. 1995. "Effectiveness Management Styles: An Indian Study." *Journal of Euro-Asian Management* 1, no. 1, pp. 43–46, 39.

# CHAPTER 4

# Management Systems

## Introduction

A management system refers to what an organization does to manage its structures, processes, activities, and resources in order that its products or services meet the organization's objectives, such as satisfying the customer's quality requirements, complying with regulations, and/or meeting environmental objectives. Elements of a management system include policy, planning, implementation and operations, performance assessment, improvement, and management review. By systemizing the way it does things, an organization can increase efficiency and effectiveness, make sure that nothing important is left out of the process and ensure that everyone is clear about who is responsible for doing what, when, how, why, and where. While all organizations should benefit from some form of management system, they are particularly important for larger organizations or ones with complicated processes. Management systems have been used for a number of years in sectors such as aerospace, automobiles, defense, and health care.

Organizations implement management systems for a variety of reasons such as achieving business objectives, increasing understanding of current operations and the likely impact of change, communicating knowledge, demonstrating compliance with legal requirements and/or industry standards, establishing "best practice," ensuring consistency, setting priorities, or changing behavior. Organizations often have more than one management system to deal with different activities or assets and integrate several related operational areas. For example, a customer relationship management system ("CRM") might be launched to manage relationships with customers. A preventive maintenance management ("PMM") and financial management systems may be used to preserve the value of organizational assets and human resource management systems merge and integrate the principles of human resource management with information technology. Other management systems focus on managing all relevant areas of operation in relation to a specific aspect such as quality, environment, health and safety, information technology, data security, corporate social responsibility, risk management, and business continuity.

Even though they may not realize it, all organizations have some sort of management system—"the way things get done"—in place. Elements of the system may be documented in the form of policies and checklists, but much of the system is based on unwritten rules and customs. The interest of organizational leaders in management systems is based not only on the desire to understand how things are currently done but also to find out how "things should be done" in order to improve organizational performance. Fortunately, reference can be made to management system standards, such as those promulgated by the International Organization for Standardization ("ISO") (www.iso.org), which are intended to provide all organizations with easy access to international "state-of-the-art" models that they can follow in implementing their own management systems. Management systems standards are concerned with processes, meaning the way that organizations go about carrying out their required work—they are not product and service standards, although processes certainly impact the quality of the organization's final products and services.

Many of the ISO standards are intended to be generic, which means that they can be applied to any organization, large or small, whatever its product or service; in any sector of activity; and whether it is a business enterprise, a public administration or a government department. The standards specify the requirements for a management system (e.g., objectives, policy, planning, implementation and operation, performance assessment, improvement and management review); however, the actual format of the system must be determined by the organization itself taking into account its specific goals and the environment in which it operates. ISO standards are available for management systems covering a broad range of topics including quality (ISO 9001, discussed below), environment (ISO 14001, discussed below), medical device quality (ISO 13485), medical devise risk (ISO 14971), information security (ISO 27001 and ISO 27002), business continuity (ISO 22301), supply chain security

(ISO 28000), corporate risk (ISO 31000), food safety (ISO 22000), and management auditing (ISO 19011).

Organizations interested in improving their practices with respect to social responsibility, including engagement with their stakeholders, may refer to ISO 26000; however, ISO 26000 is not a management system standard and does not contain requirements. Instead, ISO 26000 explains the core subjects and associated issues relating to social responsibility including organizational governance, human rights, labor practices, the environment, fair operating practices, consumer issues, and community involvement and development. For each core subject, information is provided on its scope, including key issues; its relationship to social responsibility; related principles and considerations; and related actions and expectations. For example, with respect to labor practices, one of the core subjects, organizations are reminded to integrate consideration of the following issues into their policies, organizational culture, strategies and operations: employment and employment relationships; conditions of work and social protection; social dialogue; health and safety at work; and human development and training in the workplace.[1]

As discussed below, organizations may, and often do, seek and obtain certification by independent outside parties that their management systems conform to the requirements of ISO standards. In lieu of certification, or in preparation for a certification audit, organizations should conduct formal self-assessments on a regular basis that cover quality management system requirements; management responsibility requirements; resource management requirements; product realization requirements (e.g., planning, determination of customer requirements, design and

---

[1] See International Organization for Standardization, ISO 26000 Guidance on Social Responsibility: Discovering ISO 26000 (2014) and Handbook for Implementers of ISO 26000, Global Guidance Standard on Social Responsibility by Small and Medium Sized Businesses (Middlebury, VT: ECOLOGIA, 2011). For further discussion of ISO 26000, see "Sustainability Governance and Management" prepared and distributed by the Sustainable Entrepreneurship Project (www.seproject.org).

development, purchasing, production, and service provision); and measurement, analysis, and improvement requirements.[2]

## Guidelines for Establishing a Management System

Implementing any management system, regardless of the system's particular focus (e.g., quality, environment, and risk), is a challenging task. In many cases, reference can be made to published management systems standards available from ISO and others; however, there are certain key activities that should always be considered:

- Identifying and understanding the organizational context
- Ensuring that senior management provides leadership in developing and implementing the system
- Developing a plan for the system that incorporates the risks and opportunities that could influence the performance of the system
- Ensuring that the organization is committed to support the system with the necessary internal and external resources
- Developing, planning, documenting, implementing, and controlling the organizations' operational processes
- Planning in advance for monitoring, measuring, analyzing, and evaluating the performance of the system

The following sections illustrate how the activities listed earlier might be carried out in connection with the implementation of a quality management system ("QMS").[3] In that situation, the parties responsible for implementation will typically consult and follow the standards in ISO 9001, which is described elsewhere in this chapter.

---

[2]  See http://cw.routledge.com/textbooks/eresources/9781856176842/Requirement_checklist.pdf

[3]  Portions of the discussion of implementing a quality management system in these sections have been adapted from "ISO 9001 2015–Plain English Outline" available at http://praxiom.com/iso-9001-outline.htm (accessed December 17, 2018).

# Organizational Context

Before establishing a QMS it is essential to identify and understand the organizational context by considering both the external and internal issues that are relevant to the organization's purpose and strategic direction and thinking about the influence these issues could have on its QMS and the results it intends to achieve. An effort needs to be made to monitor information about the organizational context and the impact that changes in context should be considered.

Management must also identify the interested parties who affect or could affect the QMS including parties that affect or could affect the organization's ability to provide products and services that meet customer requirements and statutory and regulatory requirements. Once the parties have been identified, management must monitor and review information about each of them in order to clarify and understand their unique needs and expectations.

Management must define the scope of the QMS by clarifying boundaries and thinking about what the QMS should apply to and then using the boundary and applicability information to define the scope. When defining the scope of the QMS, management should take into account the organizational context of the organization. Management should create a scope document for the QMS that describes the boundaries of the SMS, explains what the QMS applies to, identifies the types of products and services that will be included the QMS, and makes it clear that every ISO 9001 requirement must be applied unless an exception can be adequately asserted. Once the scope document is created procedures should be followed to maintain and control it.

Once the scope document is completed the next step is to actually develop a process-based QMS and establish documented information. Management should determine the processes that the QMS needs, the methods needed to manage processes, the resources needed to support the processes, process, responsibilities and authorities, the risks and responsibilities for each process and the methods needed to evaluate the processes. The QMS should also provide for maintenance and control of the documents required to support process operations and retention and control of the records that can be used to show that the plans are being followed. Once the QMS has been implemented and the organization is applying the criteria and methods needed to operate and control the QMS processes, provision should be made for maintaining and improving the QMS.

## Leadership

Senior management must provide leadership for the QMS initiative by focusing on quality and customers and ensuring that an appropriate quality policy is established and implemented. Leadership includes accepting responsibility for the QMS and demonstrating and communicating a commitment to QMS by explaining why quality management is important, making it clear that managers are expected to be accountable for the QMS and encouraging everyone in the organization to support the QMS and their roles in quality management. Senior management must also make it clear to everyone in the organization that emphasis on quality management emerges from the need and desire to focus on customers and that all personnel are expected to manage all relevant requirements, risks and opportunities and focus on enhancing customer satisfaction. Senior management should be closely involved in the development, establishment and implementation of the QMS and the associated policies and procedures to ensure that the QMS supports the organization's purpose, deals with the organization's context, has all requirements built into processes, and achieves all intended results. Once the QMS is ready for implementation senior management must be sure that it is fully documented and be actively involved in communicating the policies to everyone in the organization and making sure that everyone's role, responsibility, and authority with respect to the policies has been assigned and communicated.

## Planning

When planning for the development of the QMS consideration must be given to identifying the risks and opportunities that could influence the performance of the QMS or disrupt its operation and how the organizational context could affect how well the QMS is able to achieve its intended results. With this information the QMS can incorporate risk treatment options and define actions that will be taken to address the relevant risks and opportunities. The QMS should include quality objectives for all relevant areas and those objectives should be documented, communicated, monitored, and updated as necessary. Provisions should be made in advance for evaluation of the results from operation of the QMS and information from the evaluation should be used to plan and implement changes in the QMS. Whenever changes are to be made in the QMS it is essential to plan them carefully and consider the purpose of the changes, responsibilities and authorities, the potential consequences of the changes, the available of resources required to make the changes, and the impact that the changes might have on the overall integrity of the QMS.

## Resources and Support

In order for any QMS to be effective it must be supported by the necessary internal and external resources. The first requirement is making sure that the organization has access to suitable personnel who can operate and control the QMS processes. The second requirement is a suitable infrastructure that enables and supports process operations and achieving conformity of products and services. Other necessary resources include an appropriate environment for the processes and monitoring, measuring, and traceability resources.

Management needs to provide several types of support in order for the QMS to be effective and provide value to the organization. For example, management needs to be sure that the persons involved in activities that impact quality are competent and understand their roles in implementing the QMS. Competence should be documented and evaluated and appropriate training should be made available. Personnel should be made aware of the QMS and its core goals and objectives and management should share relevant information with personnel in order to allow them to carry out their jobs in a way that is consistent with the QMS goals and objectives. Another area where support is crucial is the creating and control of documentation regarding the QMS.

Documentation requirements should be consistent with key activities associated with development and commercialization of products and services and documents should be properly formatted and presented and controlled in a manner that allows for appropriate access when necessary for evaluation of the overall QMS initiative. Procedures should also be implemented covering modification to QMS documentation and protection and preservation of QMS documentation and records.

## Operations

Since so many aspects of a QMS relate to operational activities it is essential for management to carefully and thoughtfully develop, plan, document, implement, and control the organization's operational processes. Key steps in this area include:

- Determining and documenting product and service requirements, a process that should include communications with customers;
- Establishing an appropriate process to design and develop products and services, a process which should include consideration of design and development process stages and controls, complexities, requirements, expectations, participation, interfaces, resources, responsibilities, and documentation;
- Monitoring and controlling external processes, products, and services, a process that should include establishing controls for external products and services and communications with external providers to develop/clarify requirements;
- Managing and controlling production and service provision activities, a process which includes implementing controlled conditions for production, service provision, delivery processes, and post-delivery processes; and
- Controlling nonconforming outputs and document actions taken, a process that involves identifying and controlling nonconforming output to prevent unintended use and documenting nonconforming outputs and the actions that are taken.

# Evaluation and Improvement

While every effort should be made to make the QMS as effective as possible from the very beginning, the need to make changes and improvements as times goes by is inevitable. Quality management is a continuous process and companies need to plan in advance for monitoring, measuring, analyzing, and evaluating the performance of the QMS. Evaluation mechanisms should be considered during the initial planning phase of the QMS and management must ensure that the QMS includes methods for monitoring how well the needs and expectations of customers are being served. Once the data and other information from the monitoring process have been collected and measured the next step is to conduct an internal audit of the QMS in order to get a clearer picture of the suitability, adequacy, effectiveness, and direction of the QMS. Results from customer surveys and the internal audit should be used to identify new ways to enhance customer satisfaction and otherwise meet customer requirements. In addition, attention must be paid to correcting deficiencies in the way that the organization is implementing the QMS. All changes to, and corrective actions relating to, the QMS should be documented and progress should be carefully monitored through the date of the next scheduled evaluation and audit. Senior management should be thoroughly conversant in the evaluation process and should make regular presentations on the QMS to members of the board of directors.

# ISO 9001 and Quality Management Systems

ISO 9001 is one of the best known and widely used standards of the ISO and provides a structure [i.e., a "quality management system" ("QMS")] to help organizations develop products and services that consistently ensure customer satisfaction and continuously improve their products, services, and process. Quality refers to all those features of a product or service which are required by the customer. Quality management means what an organization does to ensure that its products or services satisfy the customer's quality requirements and comply with any regulations applicable to those products or services. Quality management also means what the organization does to enhance customer satisfaction and achieve continual improvement of its performance. ISO 9001 gives the requirements for what the organization must do to manage processes affecting the quality of its final products and services using Deming's "plan, do, check and improve" approach; however, ISO 9001 is not a product or service standard, nor does it specify what the objectives of the organization should be with respect to "quality" or "meeting customer requirements," each of which must be defined by organizations on their own.

ISO publications have listed a number of potential benefits for organizations electing to follow the standards and practices set out in ISO 9001[4]:

- International, expert consensus on state-of-the-art practices for quality management
- Common language for dealing with customers and suppliers worldwide in business-to-business transactions
- Increased efficiency, productivity, and effectiveness due to alignment of processes
- Model for continuous improvement
- Model for satisfying customers and other stakeholders
- Meet the necessary statutory and regulatory requirements
- Build quality into products and services from design onwards
- Identify and address the risks associated with the organization
- Address environmental concerns of customers and public and comply with government regulations
- Integrate with world economy
- Expand into new markets
- Sustainable business
- Unifying base for industry sectors
- Qualify suppliers for global supply chains
- Technical support for regulations
- Transfer of good practice to developing countries
- Tools for new economic players
- Regional integration
- Facilitate rise of services

---

[4] See the ISO publications "Overview of ISO 9001 and ISO 14001" and "ISO 9001:2015," each of which is available at the ISO website (www.iso.org).

Other potential benefits to organizations include providing senior management with better tools for implementing and maintaining an efficient management process, highlighting deficiencies and continuous assessment and improvement; clarifying areas of responsibility across all parts of the organization; communicating a positive message to employees and customers; time savings and cost reduction; and sales and marketing opportunities, including the ability to tender for new public sector projects. Organizations will also benefit from being able to provide improved quality and service, as well as "on time" delivery, to customers and reductions in the volume of returned products and customer complaints. Moreover, as customers learn more about the organization's commitment to quality, including independent audits for certification purposes, they will become more loyal to the organization and be more open to expanding the scope of the business relationship.

While not a requirement of ISO 9001, organizations may opt for ISO 9001 certification, known in some countries as registration, which means that an independent, external body conducts an audit of the organization's management system and verifies that it conforms to the requirements specified in ISO 9001. ISO itself does not carry out certification and does not issue or approve certificates. It is important that the certification body be accredited, which means that a specialized accreditation body has formally endorsed the certification body as being competent to carry out ISO 9001 certification in specified business sectors. When organizations are certified by accredited certification bodies they receive an accredited certificate, which is typically considered to carry greater weight and credibility in the marketplace. As with certifications, ISO does not carry out or approve accreditations.

As noted earlier, there is no certification requirement in ISO 9001 and companies often implement and benefit from management systems based on ISO 9001 without incurring the additional expense of going through the certification process. However, an organization may be driven to pursue certification for important business reasons such as satisfying contractual, regulatory, or market requirements; meeting customer expectations and preferences; strengthen a risk management program; and/or motivating managers and employees by establishing clear performance goals and objectives. According to ISO, over one million ISO 9001 certificates were issued across 187 countries in 2013 alone.

ISO 9001 is one of several standards in the ISO 9000 series and notice should also be taken of the following:

- ISO 9000 contains detailed explanations of the seven quality management principles with tips on how to ensure these are reflected in the way that organizations work, and also contains many of the terms and definitions used in ISO 9001.
- ISO 9004 provides guidance to organizations on how to achieve sustained success with their quality management systems.
- ISO 9011 gives guidance to organizations on performing both internal and external audits to ISO 9001 and can be used to measure the effectiveness of the quality management system and prepare for the external audit needed in order to achieve ISO 9001 certification.

## ISO 14001 and Environmental Management Systems

ISO 14001 is an internationally agreed standard that sets out the requirements for a structure [i.e., an environmental management system ("EMS")] to help organizations manage and minimize their environmental impacts, conform to applicable legal requirements, and improve their environmental performance through more efficient use of resources and reduction of waste, thereby gaining a competitive advantage and the trust of stakeholders.[5] An EMS helps organizations identify, manage, monitor, and control their environmental issues in a holistic manner and also includes the need for continual improvement of an organization's systems and approach to environmental concerns. ISO 14001, which was recently revised effective in 2015, is suitable for organizations of all types and sizes, be they private, not-for-profit, or governmental, and requires that an organization consider all environmental issues relevant to its operations, such as air pollution, water and sewage issues, waste management, soil contamination, climate change mitigation and adaptation, and resource use and efficiency.

---

[5] The summary discussion of ISO 14001 herein is adapted from "Introduction to ISO 14001: 2015" prepared and distributed by the International Organization for Standardization in 2015.

While an EMS may be adopted as a standalone system, it is often added to an existing management system (e.g., a system based on quality, such as ISO 9001). Having an EMS does not mean that an organization will be immune from all environmental challenges; however, the procedures implemented as part of an EMS should allow the organization to manage events and operational activities that will have a significant impact on the environment. ISO 14001 gives the requirements for what the organization must do to manage processes affecting the impact of its activities on the environment; however, ISO 14001 is not a product or service standard.

Organizations that have adopted and implemented ISO 14001 standards have reported that it has helped demonstrate compliance with current and future statutory and regulatory requirements; increase leadership involvement and engagement of employees; improve company reputation and the confidence of stakeholders through strategic communication; achieve strategic business aims by incorporating environmental issues into business management; provide a competitive and financial advantage through improved efficiencies and reduced costs; and encourage better environmental performance of suppliers by integrating them into the organization's business systems. There is no requirement that organizations seek and obtained accredited certification to ISO 14001 and there are many benefits from using the standard without going through the accredited certification process. However, third-party certification, which involves an audit of organizational practices against the requirements of ISO 14001 by an independent certification body (ISO does not perform certifications), has been found to be an excellent way for organizations to assure their stakeholders that the standards have been implemented correctly. Accredited certification may also be necessary for organizations to fulfill regulatory or contractual requirements.

## Elements of an EMS

In general, an EMS that is to be based on ISO 14001 standards should include the following elements[6]:

---

[6] ISO 14001. November 2000. *Environmental Management System Self-Assessment Checklist*, 2. Washington DC: Global Environmental Management Initiative. While the guidelines in the text are based on a prior version of ISO 14001,

- Development and establishment of an appropriate environmental policy that is documented and communicated to employees and also made available to the public and which includes a commitment to continual improvement and pollution prevention, regulatory compliance, and a framework for setting policy objectives;
- A planning phase that covers the identification of the environmental aspects of the organization's activities, identification and access to legal requirements, establishment and documentation of objectives and targets consistent with the and establishment of a program for achieving said targets and objectives (including the designation of responsible individuals, necessary means, and timelines);
- Implementation and operation of the EMS including the definition, documentation and communication of roles and responsibilities, provision of appropriate training, assurance of adequate internal and external communication, written management system documentation as well as appropriate document control procedures, documented procedures for operational controls, and documented and communicated emergency response procedures;
- Checking and corrective action procedures, including procedures for regular monitoring and measurement of key characteristics of the operations and activities, procedures for dealing with situations of non-conformity, specific record maintenance procedures, and procedures for auditing the performance of the EDS; and
- Periodic management reviews of the overall EMS to ensure its suitability, adequacy, and effectiveness in light of changing circumstances.

Diagnostic questions for each of these elements are included in the following sections.[7]

---

they remain relevant as an overview of how organizations should approach the process of fulfilling the ISO 14001 standards.

[7] Id.

# Environmental Policy

- Has top management defined the organization's environmental policy, ensuring that it is defined within the scope of the EMS?
- Is the policy appropriate to the nature, scale, and environmental impacts of the activities to be undertaken?
- Does the policy include a commitment to continual improvement and prevention of pollution; a commitment to comply with applicable legal and other requirements to which the organization subscribes and which relate to its environmental aspects; and a framework for setting and reviewing environmental objectives and targets?
- Is the policy documented, implemented, and maintained; communicated to all persons working for or on behalf of the organization; and available to the public?

# Planning

- Has a procedure(s) been established, implemented, and maintained to identify the environmental aspects of the organization's activities, products, and services within the defined scope of the EMS that it can control and those that it can influence taking into account planned or new developments, or new or modified activities, products, and services?
- Has a procedure(s) been established, implemented, and maintained to determine those aspects that have or can have significant impact on the environment program (i.e., significant environmental aspects)?
- Has a procedure been established to document the information on the environmental aspects of the organization's activities, products, and services and keep it up date?
- Are the significant environmental aspects of the organization's activities, products, and services taken into account in establishing, implementing, and maintaining its EMS?
- Has a procedure been established to identify and have access to the applicable legal requirements and other requirements to

which the organization subscribes related to its environmental aspects; and determine how these requirements apply to its environmental aspects?

- Has a procedure been established to ensure that applicable legal requirements and other requirements to which the organization subscribes are taking into account in establishing, implementing, and maintaining its EMS?

- Have documented environmental objectives and targets been established for relevant functions and levels within the organization? Are the objectives and targets, where practicable, measurable; and consistent with the environmental policy and legislative requirements?

- Has a program(s) been establish that addresses the means and time-frame to achieve the environmental objectives and targets?

## Implementation and Operation

- Have specific management representative(s) been appointed with the role, responsibilities, and authority for ensuring that the EMS is implemented and maintained in accordance to the ISO14001; and reporting on the performance of the EMS for review, including recommendations for improvement to the project manager?

- Has the contractor ensured that staff or subcontractors associated with work identified with the potential to cause a significant environmental impact is (are) competent on the basis of appropriate education and training or experience? Are associated records available?

- Has the contractor identified training needs associated with its environmental aspects and its EMS and provided training or taken other action to meet these needs? Are associated records available?

- Has a procedure been developed to ensure that persons working for the contractor or on its behalf are aware of the importance of conforming with the environmental policy, procedures, and requirements of the EMS; the significant environmental aspects and related actual/potential impacts associated with their work and the benefits of improved performance; their roles and responsibilities in achieving conforming with the requirements of the EMS; and the potential consequences of not following procedures?

- Has a procedure been developed for internal communications and receiving, documenting, and responding to communication from external interested parties?

- Is the level of documentation considered sufficient to describe the EMS, how its parts work together, and does it provide direction on where to obtain more detailed information on the operation of specific parts of the EMS?

- Has a procedure been developed and maintained to approve documents for adequacy prior to use; review and update as necessary and re-approve documents; addresses the changes to the format of the documents; ensure that changes and the current revision status of documents are identified; ensure that relevant versions of applicable documents are available at points of use; ensure that documents remain legible and readily identifiable; ensure that documents of external origin necessary for planning and operation of the EMS are identified and distribution controlled; and prevent the use of obsolete documents and suitable identification if they are retained for any purpose?

- Have operations that are associated with significant environmental aspects been identified and planned for by preparing procedures to ensure that they are carried out under specified conditions to control situations where their absence could lead to deviation from the environmental policy, objectives, and targets; and stipulating operating criteria?

- Has a procedure been developed to identify potential emergency situations or accidents that can have an impact on the environment and does it address how to respond to them? Does the procedure address the periodic testing where practicable?

# Checking

- Has a procedure been developed to monitor and measure key operations of the project that can have a significant environmental impact? Does the procedure include documenting information to monitor performance; the applicable operational controls; and conformity with environmental objectives and targets?
- Has a procedure been developed to evaluate compliance with applicable legal requirements and other requirements to which it subscribes?
- Has a procedure been developed to deal with actual and potential nonconformity(s) and for taking corrective action and preventative action? Does the procedure address identifying and correcting nonconformity(s) and taking action(s) to mitigate their environmental impacts; investigating nonconformity(s), determining their cause(s) and taking actions in order to avoid their recurrence; evaluating the need for action(s) to prevent nonconformity(s) and implementing appropriate actions designed to avoid their occurrence; recording the results of corrective action(s) and preventive action(s) taken; and reviewing the effectiveness of corrective action(s) and preventive action(s) taken?
- Has a procedure been developed to establish and maintain records as necessary to determine conformity to the requirements of its EMS, ISO14001 and the results achieved?
- Are internal audits to be scheduled at defined intervals to determine whether the EMS conforms to planned arrangements of environmental management including the requirements of ISO 14001; and is being properly maintained?

## Best Practices for EMS implementation

A report prepared by consultants from the Rand Corporation on the keys to successfully implementing environmental management found that it was important for organizations to integrate its environmental management program with the management system it uses to plan and execute its core missions and functions. In this way, managers would view environmental issues as being just one more relevant context in which they pursued the core values of the organization.[8] The report suggested that insights gained from surveying the best commercial practices indicated that successful and effective integration could be achieved by taking the following steps:

- Identify how environmental issues affect its key stakeholders and how these issues relate to stakeholder goals;
- Develop and sustain senior leadership support for proactive treatment of environmental issues;
- Identify champions who can take day-to-day responsibility for managing environmental issues to satisfy the specific stakeholder goals that the senior leadership has endorsed;
- Make environmental principals in the organization effective partners in coalitions in the organization to align environmental interests with other specialized interests;
- After identifying the organization's position in the value chains that it services, work with other elements of these value chains to achieve common goals;
- State specific environmental goals in simple terms that help individual decision makers relate them to broader corporate goals without much ambiguity;
- For specific decisions or projects, use teams that include representatives of all the relevant functions, including environmental representatives when appropriate;
- Promote routine use of databases and analytic tools that help decision makers see how environmental decisions affect all parts of the organization; and
- Balance centralization and decentralization to align environmental concerns with the most closely related core activities.

---

[8] Camm, F., J. Drezner, B. Lachman, and S. Resetar. 2001. *Implementing Proactive Environmental Management: Lessons Learned from Best Commercial Practice*, xii–xiii. Arlington, VA: National Defense Research Institute/RAND.

The report emphasized that while it was important to have champions and principals within the organization who could be held responsible for implementation of environmental policies in the context of the organization's broader corporate goals and culture, they must be prepared to reach out to others throughout the organization and communicate with them using data and language that can be easily understood to demonstrate how their interests can be aligned with the environmental mission. The report also provided the following recommendations for implementing a proactive approach to environmental management[9]:

- Motivate employees to be not only creative but also dogged in their determination to change the status quo for the better;
- Assign responsibilities clearly so that specific individuals or teams feel the effects of environmental decisions on the organization as a whole and can be held accountable for promoting the goals of the organization as a whole over the long term;
- Design metrics to encourage individuals and teams, constrained as they are in their particular locations in the organization, to make decisions compatible with the organization's broad goals;
- Back up these metrics with incentives that are compatible with the organization's broader norms about compensation and advancement;
- Expect individual failures to occur when employees push hard enough for real change and (1) limit the damage from such failures while (2) helping employees learn from these failures rather than punishing them for failing;
- Train employees to increase their environmental awareness and improve their ability to work collaboratively;
- Design training so that it occurs "just in time," when employees need it to execute specific tasks;
- Provide effective analytic tools and maintain a supportive organizational environment for their use;

---

[9] Id. at pp. xiv–xv.

- Communicate continuously, internally and with key stake-holders, to sustain trust and commitment; and
- Benchmark environmental performance against that of other organizations, report the results to the senior leadership, and use the results to sustain senior-level support for continuing improvement in environmental performance.

Companies often implement several different, but interrelated, environmental management programs as part of their overall environmental strategy. Common areas of focus include product design, which involves continuous efforts of design teams to locate new materials and technologies to ensure that future products are at the leading edge of commercial environmental product design and recognition of specific design considerations such as environmentally oriented materials selection, design to facilitate cleaner production, design for durability and extended product life, design for refurbishment and reuse and design for disassembly and recycling; supply chain management, which involves routine dialog with supply chain members about their efforts to create and maintain a sustainable production system and adhere to environmental requirements through continuous improvement actions; operations, including certification of the company's EMS; product stewardship, including a robust and practical end-of-life management approach that maximizes environmental and economic value; and communications with internal and external stakeholders regarding sustainability.[10]

## ISO 45001 and Environmental, Health and Safety Management Systems

An important tool for companies seeking to implement environmental, health and safety ("EH&S") management systems was introduced by ISO in 2018 when the new ISO 45001 standard on occupational health and safety management systems was finalized and published. ISO 45001 is intended to help organizations reduce the burden of occupational

---

[10] Sustainable Business: A Handbook for Starting a Business (New Zealand Trade and Enterprise).

accidents and illnesses by providing a framework to improve employee safety, reduce workplace risks and create better, safer working conditions, all over the world. ISO 45001 follows other generic management system approaches such as ISO 14001 and ISO 9001 and also takes into account other relevant internal standards such as OHSAS 18001 (an international standard that has provided a framework to identify, control, and decrease the risks associated with health and safety within the workplace), the International Labour Organization's ILO-OSH Guidelines, various national standards and the ILO's comprehensive international labor standards and conventions.[11]

The ISO has explained that an occupational health and safety ("OH&S") management system is intended to support organizations in meeting their responsibilities with respect to the occupational health and safety of workers and others who can be affected by its activities. An effective OH&S management system enables organizations to provide safe and healthy workplaces, prevent work-related injury and ill health, and continually improve its OH&S performance. The ISO has made it clear that implementation of an OH&S management system is a strategic and operational decision for an organization, and that the implementation and maintenance of an OH&S management system, its effectiveness and its ability to achieve its intended outcomes are dependent on a number of key factors, which can include[12]:

- Top management leadership, commitment, responsibilities, and accountability;
- Top management developing, leading, and promoting a culture in the organization that supports the intended outcomes of the OH&S management system;
- Communication;

---

[11] It is anticipated that ISO 45001 will replace OHSAS 18001 within three years of the March 2018 publication date of ISO 45001, thus organizations relying on external standards for creating their EH&S management systems should refer to the requirements and recommendations of ISO 45001 rather than OHSAS 18001.

[12] https://iso.org/obp/ui/#iso:std:iso:45001:ed-1:v1:en

- Consultation and participation of workers, and, where they exist, workers' representatives;
- Allocation of the necessary resources to maintain it;
- OH&S policies, which are compatible with the overall strategic objectives and direction of the organization;
- Effective process(es) for identifying hazards, controlling OH&S risks and taking advantage of OH&S opportunities;
- Continual performance evaluation and monitoring of the OH&S management system to improve OH&S performance;
- Integration of the OH&S management system into the organization's business processes;
- OH&S objectives that align with the OH&S policy and take into account the organization's hazards, OH&S risks and OH&S opportunities; and
- Compliance with its legal requirements and other requirements.

EHS Support, which provides a wide array of EH&S services and support to clients across a broad spectrum of industries, has laid out the following list of essential elements for an effective HS&E management system[13]:

- *Management Leadership, Commitment, and Accountability*: The board of directors, the EH&S committee of the board and the senior management team must take responsibility for establishing policy, providing perspective, setting expectations, and ensuring the provision of adequate resources for successful operations. Management leadership, commitment, and action need to be visible to the organization, and clear accountabilities must be established at all levels.
- *Risk Planning, Assessment, and Management*: Risk planning, assessment, and management is a continuous process that

[13] Adapted from Statement of Environment, Health and Safety Policy issued by Kenny Ogilvie. "CEO of EHS Support." on August 24, 2012, http://ehs-support.com/wp-content/uploads/EHSMS-Manual.pdf (accessed December 17, 2018).

includes the formal and informal identification, evaluation, and control of EH&S business risks including business liabilities, regulatory compliance, and customer requirements.

- *Facility/Site and Equipment/Tool Safety Management*: Safety can be enhanced and risk to health and the environment can be minimized by using effective standards, procedures, and management systems for facility/site design, activities, and services. Health and safety plans should be used to summarize health and safety hazard information for field activities.

- *EH&S Regulatory Management, Information, and Documentation*: Accurate information about the configuration and capabilities of sites and facilities, properties of products and materials handled, potential hazards, and regulatory requirements is essential to assess and manage risk. All projects and services should comply with the organization's regulatory compliance procedures and contractors should be required to have equivalent procedures in place and submit to audits of such procedures by the organization.

- *EH&S Planning and Procedures*: Safety and health policies and programs should be established and maintained to manage significant risks and comply with legal requirements. All such policies and programs should be written, communicated and followed, and be accessible to personnel, contractors, and government entities as appropriate.

- *Personnel, Organization, Competence, and Training*: Recognizing that people are at the core of every EH&S initiative, provision must be made for appropriate training, effective communication and assessment of employees, and the implementation of appropriate programs.

- *Emergency Management and Community Awareness*: The organization must take a proactive rather than reactive approach to planning and preparing for a safe and effective emergency response to incidents that mitigate the consequences, prevents further harm and enables a safe efficient resumption of normal operations. In the event of an incident, plans must be in place to ensure that all necessary actions are taken for the protection of the public, the environment, and organizational personnel and assets.

- *Incident Investigation, Analysis, and Management*: While every effort should be made to prevent incidents, the reality is that problems will arise and the organization must be committed to effectively managing all incidents, including work-related injuries, accidents, regulatory violations, and near misses, immediately and thoroughly and communicating the results of investigations and following proper reporting practices.
- *Management of Change*: Changes in services, procedures, site standards, facilities, or personnel must be evaluated and managed to ensure that risks arising from these changes are properly assessed and managed.
- *Third Party Services*: Third parties (e.g., contractors and contracted personnel working directly with or for the organization and suppliers) impact the organization's business and reputation and it is essential that they perform in a manner that is consistent and compatible with the EH&S policies, procedures, and expectations of the organization.
- *EH&S Performance Monitoring, Measurement, Reporting, & Improvement*: To ensure continuous improvement, EH&S performance must be accurately monitored, measured, recorded, and analyzed, with the key tools being audits, review and self-assessments with respect to achievement of EH&S plan and objectives; compliance with federal, state, and local regulations; corrective actions closeout; and leading and lagging indicators. Provision should be made for continuous review of EH&S systems and continuous improvement implementation. In addition, systems should be implemented for, and adequate resources allocated to, reporting of EH&S performance to stakeholders.

## Enterprise Risk Management

No business is without some sort of risk and overcoming those risks is the key to achieving an acceptable return on investment of capital, technology, and human resources. Higher levels of risk drive investors to expect greater risk-adjusted returns in exchanging for providing capital to the business. The risk profile for each company is different; however, commentators have suggested that the range of risks confronting an enterprise may appear within an extensive list that includes the following, in no particular order: financial markets disruption; credit; interest rate; capital; human resources; transactional; data protection and privacy; legal; enforcement actions by federal or state criminal authorities; Foreign Corrupt Practices Act; governmental investigations; regulatory and compliance requirements; cyberattacks; information technology; business continuity and disaster planning; operational; supply chain; financial disclosure; document retention policies and practices and disclosure (obstruction of justice or civil contempt); executive misconduct or negligence (personal and/or professional); brand; reputational; vendors; business partners; third party service providers; customers; and environmental.[14]

The scope of the potential risks to a company above should illustrate why companies need a formalized approach to risk management, systems and programs that have come to be known as "enterprise risk management," or "ERM." ERM programs, which often include compliance aspects or are implemented in conjunction with a separate but related compliance program, have been mandated or highly recommended by federal and state laws and regulations, such as the Sarbanes-Oxley Act of 2002 and the Dodd-Frank Wall Street Reform and Consumer Protection Act; federal sentencing guidelines; listing standards required by national securities exchanges; credit agencies; directors' and officers' liability insurance carriers; and accounting and audit review standards. In many cases, companies are required, or strongly urged, to create a separate board-level risk management committee and appoint a chief risk officer. ERM has been conceived as a comprehensive solution to risk management that

---

[14] Goldberg, G., and M. McNamara. n.d. "Effective Enterprise Risk Management and Crisis Management: Roles and Responsibilities of the Board and Management." https://dentons.com/en/insights/alerts/2012/august/20/effective-enterprise-risk-management-and-crisis-management (accessed on August 20, 2012).

requires that all strategic, management, and operational tasks of an organization be enabled through projects, functions, and processes so that those tasks are aligned to a common set of risk management objectives. ERM addresses various types of risk exposures including[15]:

- Hazard risk risks related to accidental losses, such as workplace injuries, liability torts, property damage, and natural disasters
- Financial risk risks related to financial activities, such as pricing, asset valuation, currency fluctuations, and liquidity
- Operational risk risks related to operations, such as supply chain, customer satisfaction, product failure, or loss of key personnel
- Strategic risk risks related with an organization's long-term goals and management, such as partnerships, mergers, and acquisitions
- Reputational risk risks related to the trustworthiness of business (damage to a firm's reputation can result in lost revenue or destruction of shareholder value)
- Compliance risk risks related to violations of or nonconformance with laws, rules, regulations, prescribed practices, internal policies, and procedures, or ethical standards.

Apart from legal and regulatory requirements, companies have recognized that ERM can be deployed as an essential business management tool to assess and analyze business and activities on a risk-adjusted basis; engage in sound strategic planning and financial management which requires that all risks of every line of business and activity be assessed and balanced against profitability, and recognize and prepare for the interdependency of events.[16]

---

[15] Risk Managers are from Mars, EHS Professionals are from Venus: The EHS Professionals' Role in ERM (California State University Risk Management Authority).

[16] Goldberg, G., and M. McNamara. n.d. "Effective Enterprise Risk Management and Crisis Management: Roles and Responsibilities of the Board and

The first step in creating an ERM program is conducting an enterprise-wide risk identification and assessment program, preferably undertaken by an independent third party and with the intent that the assessment process would be continuously updated on a regular basis. The goal of the risk assessment, which is discussed in more detail below, is to create a solid foundation for designing an ERM program that is aligned with the most material risks confronting the organization. Once the assessment has been completed the results should be reviewed by the board of directors and the senior management of the company and specialists should be assigned to develop a proposal for the ERM program. The proposal should be reviewed by the entire board and senior management and approval of the program should be accompanied by a commitment to provide the resources necessary for the program to be successful. At this point the ERM infrastructure should also be established starting with allocation of risk topics among committees of the board and continuing with the appointment of a chief risk officer and creation of an ERM committee that will include senior representatives from each of the main functional groups of the company and the company's various business units.

While creation of a standalone committee at the board level to focus on risk management issues and initiatives is growing in popularity it is by no means a universally accepted approach. Each company must make its own decision and Deloitte has suggested that the follow factors and questions should be considered when deciding whether a risk committee at the board level is appropriate[17]:

- The needs of the stakeholders: The board should assess the quality of the current risk governance and oversight structure, the risk environment, and the future needs of the organization to determine how best to meet the needs of all of the company's stakeholders, not just investors.

- Alignment of risk governance with strategy: Having a risk-focused committee at the board level increases the likelihood that the board, management, and business units be aligned with their approach to risk and strategy, this promoting better risk governance and ensures that risk oversight is value-adding.

- Oversight of the risk management infrastructure: The decisions about the role of the board-level committee, if any, should be made in the context of larger questions regarding who will be in charge of the people, processes, and resources of the risk management program. Assuming that a chief risk officer position will be created, it is important to be clear about reporting obligations for that position (e.g., to the risk committee, the entire board, or the CEO).

- Scope of risk committee responsibilities: Before a board-level committee is formed decisions must be about the scope of its responsibilities. In some cases the committee may be responsible for overseeing all risks; however, the board may decide that certain risks should be primarily addressed by other committees (e.g., the audit committee should maintain oversight of risks associated with financial reporting) and that the purview of the risk committee should be limited.

- Communication among committees: Particularly when the scope of the responsibilities of the risk committee are to be limited as mentioned earlier, the board must clear define boundaries among all of the board committees and establish communication channels to be sure that activities do not overlap or that important risks "fall between the cracks."

# CHAPTER 5

# Managing in Developing Countries

## Introduction

For decades the general consensus among Western policymakers involved with international economic development was that real progress was dependent on making sure that poorer countries implemented and followed "appropriate" fiscal, monetary, trade, and legal practices. While there is little dispute that national economic policies and rules are important for economic development, it has also been recognized that the managers in developing countries that have a hand in producing goods and services can have just as much impact on the pace of development.[1] It is, therefore, essential to study and understand management practices and styles in developing countries; however, while developing countries represent an overwhelmingly large percentage of the world's population, the relatively small portion of global business activities in those countries, as well as other factors, has led to a small and spotty body of research on management practices and styles in those countries.[2] One researcher lamented that while "[d]eveloping countries offer potentially some of the most important growth opportunities for companies both from the

---

[1] For an early discussion of the debate regarding the importance of "economists" versus "businesspeople" in fostering economic development, see Heller, F. 1968. "The Role of Management in Economic Development." *Management International Review* 8, no. 6, pp. 63–70.

[2] For a general introduction to the issues relating to management including the relationship between management and performance and the challenges confronting managers around the world, see "Introduction to Management Studies" prepared and distributed by the Sustainable Entrepreneurship Project (www.seproject.org).

developing as the developing world ... [reviews] ... of empirical research grounded in institutional theory [have] found that most studies focused on developed countries and that only a small portion of the studies tried to test institutional theory in developed countries."[3]

The field of management studies was conceived and developed predominantly in the United States, with some recent inputs coming from other industrialized countries in Europe and Asia (e.g., the tremendous interest in researching Japanese management practices in the 1980s and early 1990s). As such, most of management-related theories that have been produced and researched are based on circumstances in developed countries and thus include biases and assumptions that will likely make them inapplicable in developing countries. One of the problems with studying management in developing countries is that the landscape is tremendously diverse and includes countries of all sizes and from all continents and peoples who with unique histories that practice numerous religions, speak hundreds of different languages, and live in a breathtaking sweep of geographic conditions. All of this makes it difficult to formulate accurate and useful generalizations about "developing country management practices" and/or the attitudes and preferences of employees in all of those countries as to how they would like to be managed.

## Applicability of Western Management Theories to Developing Countries

One of the long-running issues within the research community focusing on developing countries has been the extent to which management theories and practices with roots in the industrialized world could be understood and effectively applied by organizational managers in

---

[3] de Waal, A. 2007. "Is Performance Management Applicable in Developing Countries?: The Case of a Tanzanian College." *International Journal of Emerging Markets* 2, no. 1, pp. 68–83, 68 (citing Farashahi, M., T. Hafso, and R. Molz. 2005. "Institutionalized Norms of Conducting Research and Social Realities: A Research Synthesis of Empirical Works from 1983 to 2002." *International Journal of Management Review* 7, no. 1, pp. 1–24).

developing countries.[4] Not surprisingly, there are several different theories on this issue including the following[5]:

- Proponents of the "divergence" perspective argue that cultural differences between societies such as those that have been identified by Hofstede and others make it difficult for Western management theories and practices to be effectively applied in non-Western societal cultures that are typically found in the developing world. Scholars holding this view also reject the notion of a universal theory of management on the grounds that cultural differences cannot be overcome.[6]
- The "universal" perspective contrasts directly and sharply with the divergence perspective and holds that applicability of management theories and practices is not limited by culture and that certain similar management practices—universal practices—can be identified in organizations all around the world regardless of the level of economic development in the location where they are operating.[7]

---

[4] Hoskisson, R., L. Eden, C. Ming Lau, and M. Wright. 2000. "Strategy in Emerging Economies." *Academy of Management Journal* 43, no. 3, pp. 249–67. For further background on the debate regarding cross-cultural transfer of US management theories to other countries, see "Comparative Management Studies" prepared and distributed by the Sustainable Entrepreneurship Project (www.seproject.org).

[5] Derived from Hafsi, T., and M. Farashahi. n.d. "Applicability of Management Theories to Developing Countries: A Synthesis." *The Free Library,* http://the-freelibrary.com/Applicability of management theories to developing countries: a...-a0141092760 (accessed on October 1, 2005).

[6] See Hofstede, G. 1994. "Cultural Constraints in Management Theories." *International Review of Strategic Management* 7, no. 1, pp. 27–49; Jaeger, A. 1990. "The Applicability of Western Management Techniques in Developing Countries: A Cultural Perspective." In *Management in Developing Countries,* eds. A. Jaeger and R. Kanungo, 131–45. London: Routlege.

[7] See Mintzberg, H. 1973. *The Nature of Managerial Work.* New York, NY: Harper & Row; Mintzberg, H. July-August 1975. "The Manager's Job-Folklore and Fact." *Harvard Business Review* 53, no. 4, p. 49; and Lubatkin, M., M. Ndiaye, and R. Vengroff. 1997. "The Nature of Managerial Work in

- The "convergence" perspective argues that applicability of management theories is correlated with the level of economic development and industrialization of a society and that the adoption of Western-style management theories by developing countries is a function of their ability to overcome technical and economic difficulties rather than cultural constraints.
- The "situational," or "contingency," theory dismisses the claims of the proponents of the universal perspective and argues that applicability of management theories will depend on situational factors such as the personality of the manager, the ownership structure of the firm, hierarchy, and whether the firm is privately or publicly owned and operated.

One of the earliest formal studies of the applicability of Western-style management theories to developing countries was conducted by Kiggundu et al. in the early 1980s and they concluded that those theories would only be applicable in situations where the organization in the developing country could behave as a closed system. In other words, when the theories related only to the core technology of an organization without reference to its external environment the theories tended to be applicable with conditions and results similar to those of organizations in developed countries; however, the theories would not be applicable in situations involving the external environment.[8]

In the decades following the publication of the Kiggundu et al. study a growing number of researchers turned their attention to empirically studying the effectiveness of attempts to introduce and implement Western managerial practices in developing countries. For example, Wood and Caldas conducted extensive research on the successes and failures

---

Developing Countries: A Limited Test of the Universalist Hypothesis." *Journal of International Business Studies* 28, no. 4, pp. 711–33.

[8] Hafsi, T., and M. Farashahi. n.d. "Applicability of Management Theories to Developing Countries: A Synthesis." *The Free Library,* http://thefreelibrary.com/ Applicability of management theories to developing countries: a...-a0141092760 (accessed on October 1, 2005).

associated with attempts to adopt imported managerial expertise into Brazil.[9] They posited a model, or framework, for understanding the integration of foreign managerial techniques in Brazil that began with various external, or contextual, factors such as the historical roots and cultural heritage of the country, particularly "plasticity" and "formalism"; contemporary external influences, including globalization and the sudden need for Brazil to transition from a feudal, agrarian economy into a player on the world economic stage; and low national competitiveness due to protectionist policies and underdeveloped productivity tools. Wood and Caldas emphasized that the two cultural traits—"plasticity" and "formalism"—significantly influenced the receptivity of Brazilians to foreign managerial techniques. On the one hand, plasticity, or an "openness and permeability to foreign influences," triggered an apparent acceptance of foreign items; however, the formalism in Brazilian societal culture meant there was a "tendency to adopt façade behaviors resulting in a discrepancy between the formal and the real," including behavior designed to deceive foreigners that alien practices were being adopted when, in fact, they were being resisted or only being partially adopted.[10] The framework also included intermediate factors, including diffusion agents (e.g., Brazilian government and its agencies, business schools, business media, and consultancies), that drove the promotion, dissemination, and legitimization of new ideas. For example, Caldas and Wood noted that initiatives to adopt imported managerial practices such as the ISO 9000 system were often driven by government programs that provided incentives to firms if they pursued ISO certification.[11]

---

[9] See Wood, T., and M. Caldas. 2002. "Adopting Imported Managerial Expertise in Developing Countries: The Brazilian Experience." *Academy of Management Executive* 16, no. 2, pp. 18–32. The description of Brazilian experiences with ISO 9000, reengineering and enterprise resource planning in the following paragraph is adapted from a discussion on page 19 of the cited article. See also Caldas, M., and T. Wood. 1997. "For the English to See: The Importation of Managerial Technology in Late 20th Century Brazil." *Organization* 4, no. 4, pp. 517–34.

[10] Wood, T., and M. Caldas. 2002. "Adopting Imported Managerial Expertise in Developing Countries: The Brazilian Experience." *Academy of Management Executive* 16, no. 2, pp. 18–22.

[11] Id. at p. 23.

Caldas and Wood found evidence that Brazilian managers perceived programs and projects based on ISO certification to be irrelevant and/or inappropriate and that efforts to develop ISO systems actually raised costs and contributed to organizational rigidity because the conditions that existed in Brazilian firms were not favorable to such systems (i.e., poorly skilled laborers, high power distance, and highly centralized decision-making processes). Reengineering programs launched in Brazil during the mid- and late-1990s also yielded minimal benefits, which Wood and Caldas blamed on a failure to take into account organizational culture, competencies, and strategies. Other unexpected and damaging consequences of reengineering in Brazil flowed from the tendency of firms to use the programs as an excuse for downsizing for its own sake, rather than enhancing productivity, and this led to "loss of leadership, deterioration of organizational climate, decrease of organizational memory, reduction of productivity and efficiency, decline of perceived product and/or service quality, and hammering of organizational reputation." Finally, while the introduction of enterprise resource planning did result in some improvements with respect to integration and quality of information, gains in productivity and competitiveness were rare due to scope and planning mistakes and failure to customize the new systems to the specific organizational needs of Brazilian firms.

Wood and Caldas concluded that Brazilian firms often appeared to adopt foreign managerial practices in response to political, institutional, and substantive pressures but that cultural factors, notably formalism, and contemporary economic and social factors, such as poorly skilled workers, led to unsuccessful and unreasoned adoption of the practices with little added value.[12] Wood and Caldas had also cited the "level of critical reasoning" as an important factor in predicting the success of effectively adopting foreign managerial techniques, noting that higher levels of critical reasoning would allow local managers to critically analyze the techniques and adapt them to local conditions in a way that would increase the changes of effective integration. Wood and Callas noted that the significant political and institutional pressures in Brazil to appear to

---

[12] Id. at pp. 21 and 25.

adopt foreign methods quickly deprived local managers of the time or incentive to critically analyze the proposed solutions and the result was that "most adoptions tend to be uncritical, and the results for firms may be quite harmful."[13]

In 2005, Hafsi and Farashahi decided it was time to take a fresh look at the research that had been conducted since the Kiggundu et al. article and undertook a review of 170 articles that were published from 1983 through 2002 to test their hypothesis that, despite the findings of researchers such as Caldas and Wood, circumstances had changed and that Western-based concepts of general management and organizational theories had achieved widespread applicability in developing countries.[14] Their review led them to conclude that the "[r]esearchers working on organizations in developing countries will find a managerial behaviour that is similar to what may be seen in the developed countries." Hafsi and Farashahi suggested that their conclusions could be traced to a mix of environmental changes since the early 1980s as well as to extension of organizational theory to cover an increasing variety of circumstances and organizations.[15] In their view, the key environmental changes included the following:

- Major global political and economic institutions, such as the World Bank and the International Monetary Fund, imposed their structural adjustment framework on many emerging and developing economies.[16] While this has not necessarily

---

[13] Id. at p. 21.

[14] Hafsi, T., and M. Farashahi. n.d. "Applicability of Management Theories to Developing Countries: A Synthesis." *The Free Library*, http://thefreelibrary.com/ Applicability of management theories to developing countries: a...-a0141092760 (accessed on October 1, 2005).

[15] Farashahi, M., T. Hafsi, and R. Molz. 2005. "Institutionalized Norms of Conducting Research and Social Realities: A Research Synthesis of Empirical Works From 1983–2002." *International Journal of Management Reviews* 7, no. 1, pp. 1–24.

[16] Kamarck, A.M. 1996. "The World Bank: Challenges and Creative Responses." In *The Bretton Woods-GATT System: Retrospect and Prospect After Fifty Years*, ed. O. Kirshner, 106–27. London: M.E, Sharpe; Knoop, C.I., and G.C. Lodge. 1996.

produced the economic growth that was anticipated and desired it has been successful from a process perspective and, as a result, local institutions—governments that insisted on continuous intervention in the economy and commercial markets—have been pushed aside and replaced by growing influence of global institutions dominated by Western countries.[17] While this has sometimes caused resentment in developing countries it has also softened the view of Western management and organizational practices in those countries and they are now increasingly seen as being acceptable.[18]

- A number of events and innovations have accelerated globalization of markets, industries, and firms including reduction of tariff and non-tariff barriers, creation of the World Trade Organization and the emergence, growth, and maturation of large free trade areas (e.g., the European Union, ASEAN, and the North American Free Trade Agreement).[19]

---

"World Bank (A): Under Siege." *Harvard Business School Case*, 9–797. Boston: Harvard Business School Press; Rich, B. 1994. *Mortgaging the Earth: The World Bank, Environmental Impoverishment, and the Crisis of Development*. Boston: Beacon Press; and Wapenhans, W. 1995. *What's Ahead For the World Bank?*. MI, Flint: Charles Stewart Mott Foundation Publications.

[17] With regard to how interaction between local institutions and global ones have influenced regulators, firms, and markets in developing countries, see Carney, M., and M. Farashahi. 2006. "Transnational Institutions in Developing Countries: The Case of Iranian Civil Aviation." *Organization Studies* 27, no. 1, pp. 53–77. In general, developing countries looking to build and enhance their own capabilities in a complex and technology-driven area such as commercial airlines must be prepared to recognize and follow global regulatory schemes and managerial, technical, and security norms dictated by manufacturers and investors from Western countries.

[18] Lubatkin, M., M. Ndiaye, and R. Vengroff. 1997. "The Nature of Managerial Work in Developing Countries: A Limited Test of the Universalist Hypothesis." *Journal of International Business Studies* 28, no. 4, pp. 711–33.

[19] Doz, Y.L. 1986. *Strategic Management in Multinational Companies*. Oxford: Pergamon; and Porter, M. 1990. *The Competitive Advantage of Nations*. London: Macmillan.

- Barriers to cross-border communication have been struck down by rapid and often astonishing technological innovations thus facilitating the movement toward global uniformity of perceptions and understanding regarding fundamental financial and economic issues and potential solutions.[20]
- Most emerging and developing countries have embraced and launched privatization programs and the processes and practices of privatization have become more uniform around the world.[21]
- The rapid global growth of industries based on the application of common and complex technologies has pushed developing and emerging countries to learn and adopt the managerial rules, norms, and theories associated with those industries. This has been particularly true in instances where globalization has been led by multinational firms as has been the cases in industries such as banking and automobiles. The standardization that so often accompanies globalization has often clashed with strong local tastes and cultural constraints including religious practices; however, even in those instances multinational firms have generally found a way to make reasonable accommodations for local preferences while implementing managerial practices and administrative techniques that are quite similar in most parts of the world (e.g., automobile manufacturers use the same standards to manage production and train workers in every country where they build their products).
- More and more firms headquartered in countries around the world have adopted and implemented global growth strategies that has resulted in wider and freer access to markets, capital,

---

[20] Eisenmann, T. 2003. "High Definition TV: The Grand Alliance." *Harvard Business School Case*, 9–804, 103. Boston: Harvard Business School Press; and Henderson, R., and D. Yoffie. 2004. "Nokia and MIT's project Oxygen." *Harvard Business School Case*, 9–704, 474. Boston: Harvard Business School Press.
[21] World Development Report, 1999-2003. 2003. Washington, D.C.: World Bank Group.

human resources, and other assets and facilitated the transfer of managerial theories through actual practice in developing and emerging countries.[22] Multinational firms, in particular, have taken the lead in introducing and popularizing effective management practices that other firms, including many in developing countries, want to emulate. The practice of multinational firms of entering into joint ventures and other strategic alliances with local partners in developing countries is another way in which those firms are leading the push toward convergence in management practices.[23]

- Managing training has become more uniform and standardized around the world and developing countries in particular has experienced substantial growth in the number of formal management training programs and business schools sponsored and staffed by Western-based organizations such as the Association to Advance Collegiate Schools of Business and the Association of MBAs.[24] The result has been that managers being trained today in developing countries are more likely to be exposed to, and adopt, techniques, behavioral norms, and values that are substantially similar to those being introduced to their colleagues in the United States and other Western countries.[25]

---

[22] Doz, Y.L. 1986. *Strategic Management in Multinational Companies*. Oxford: Pergamon; and Marnet, O. 2005. "Economic Governance in the Age of Globalization." *Journal of Economic Issues* 39, no. 1, pp. 282–85.
[23] See Lee, J., T. Roehl, and S. Choe. 2000. "What Makes Management Style Similar and Distinct Across Borders? Growth, Experience and Culture in Korean and Japanese Firms." *Journal of International Business Studies* 31, no. 4, pp. 631–52.
[24] Venezia, G. 2005. "Impact of Globalization of Public Administration Practices on Hofstede's Cultural Indices." *Journal of American Academy of Business* 6, no. 2, p. 344.
[25] The spread of Western management techniques to developing countries has corresponded to the evolution of management toward more of a science than an art, a phenomenon which has led to global training practices supported by what Hafsi and Farashahi referred to as the "strong homogenizing effect of certification associations and agencies." See also Wright, P.C., and G.D. Geroy. 2003. "Is it Time for ISO-9000 Managers?" *Management Research News* 26, no. 1, pp. 41–54.

Hafsi and Farashahi argued that, taken together, the changes listed earlier had led to the development and dissemination of shared knowledge and technical language among managers around the world regardless of the level of development of the countries in which they are practicing. They also noted that the global environment for business activities had been transformed by advances in technology and elimination of trade barriers that allowed great mobility of capital, labor, and other resources and wider and freer access to markets around the world. In addition, Hafsi and Farashahi felt that these trends had reduced the traditional ability of governments in developing countries to exercise inordinate amounts of control over their local economies and had forced public officials in those countries to begin acting in the same way as their colleagues in the industrialized world and adopt policies, such as privatization, that turned responsibility for commerce and innovation over to managers in the private sector. In their words: "To restate the obvious, we claim that an important process of institutional diffusion has taken place in the last decades. It has been pushed by international agencies' regulatory processes; by powerful normative processes that have defined good economic practices, and determined the behaviour of economists and managers all over the world; and by dominant cultural-cognitive processes whereby western civilization mostly economic values take over traditional values (citations omitted)."[26]

## Impact of Emergence of Global Competitors from Developing Countries

Interest in management outside of the United States, Europe, Japan, and other Asian countries such as Korea was fueled by the emergence of new global competitors such as the so-called "BRIC countries": Brazil, Russia, India, and China, and it is now increasingly common to see articles and books comparing management practices in those countries to those used in the United States and other developed countries. In many instances, however, the primary thread of inquiry is on how US-based management

---

[26] Hafsi, T., and M. Farashahi. n.d. "Applicability of Management Theories to Developing Countries: A Synthesis." *The Free Library,* http://thefreelibrary.com/ Applicability of management theories to developing countries: a...-a0141092760 (accessed October 1, 2005).

practices, particularly in the human resources area, can be transferred to these developing economies, often with the anticipation that US multinationals will be establishing a large presence in those countries and are interested in importing their own management techniques as opposed to learning and applying indigenous practices. Many developing countries have their own body of research on local management practices compiled and recorded by academics, consultants, and policymakers in those countries—India is a particularly good example of a developing country with a substantial body of indigenous management literature; however, these materials are often difficult to access and may not have been translated to make it useful for interested parties from outside those countries.

The dichotomy between developed and developing countries, and the members of each of those groups, has a long history and has become deeply engrained in the minds of many scholars, policymakers, and ordinary citizens around the world. However, there is evidence of significant changes which, if taken to their seemingly logical conclusion, will disrupt orthodox thinking about the sources of best practices for managers and will generate new ideas among scholars researching management in developing countries. Already we are seeing large enterprises from countries still classified as "developing," such as Brazil, China, and India, involved in battles to assume ownership and managerial control over valuable economic assets in industrialized countries—and sometimes the only serious bidders are firms from the developing countries. In addition, industrialized countries are seeing progressively higher levels of inbound foreign investment from developing countries, often accompanied by a transfer of managers and their own managerial styles and practices from the investing country. Observing these events, Punnett has commented: "What literature there is on management interactions between developing and developed countries implicitly assumes that managers from developed countries will be adapting to the environment in developing countries. The reverse may be more and more the reality of the management challenges of the 21st century."[27]

---

[27] Punnett, B. n.d. "Management in Developing Countries." http://cavehill-uwi.academia.edu/BettyJanePunnett/Papers/181413/Managing_in_Developing_Countries

## Developing Countries as Testing Grounds for New Management Theories

There is no question that introduction and transfer of "foreign" management theories and practices into developing countries has been a long and challenging process that is far from ending and which has been complicated by various factors including the importance of history, values and unwritten rules, norms, and related practices that cannot be easily identified and understood by outsiders. However, globalization generally, as well as the specific factors emphasized by Hafsi and Farashahi, have become sources of change for values and institutions in developing countries and recent years have seen countries such as China, India, Korea, and Turkey willingly seek out and adapt various Western management practices in a way rarely thought to be possible in the past. As a result, Hafsi and Farashahi posited the somewhat radical suggestion that "the question, whether Western-based theoretical development is applicable to developing countries, may have become irrelevant," and then went on to explain that if one does concede that Western management theories can be effectively applied in many ways in developing countries then it was time to include those countries as part of "normal" scientific development that simply expands the diversity of contexts and circumstances in which discoveries regarding organizational structures and management can be made.

Hafsi and Farashahi predicted that developing countries may, in the future, provide novel and interesting ideas for managers in more industrialized countries, particularly as managers in the United States and Western Europe struggle to compete in fast changing and relatively unstable environments that have long been the norm in developing countries. Hafsi and Farashahi noted: "What is discovered in organizations in Texas, France or Saudi Arabia may or may not apply to organizations in Bangladesh, California or the UK; but we can at least relate the reasons to well-known concepts and theories, in particular to developments that recognize the importance of perceptions, values, beliefs and other soft influences on decision-makers' behaviour."[28] What this means is that in

---

[28] Hafsi, T., and M. Farashahi. n.d. "Applicability of Management Theories to Developing Countries: A Synthesis." *The Free Library,* http://thefreelibrary.com/

order for organizational management theory and research to be robust, timely, and useful in the future it should include study of practices in all of the geographical locations mentioned earlier coupled with rejection of the historical notion of management practices in developing countries being a degraded, or poor, form of management.

A. de Waal also expressed high hopes for the value of management studies in developing countries and argued that it could reasonably be assumed that the "highly dynamic environment ... [in these countries] ... is a good testing ground for new theory, techniques and concepts of business and management."[29] He was more cautious than Hafsi and Farashahi about the efficacy of Western management practices in emerging markets due to significant cultural differences, but pointed out that if such practices could not be easily transferred then it was imperative for management scholars all over the world to seek out new solutions to managerial issues that would suit the specific cultural, economic, and political conditions found in developing countries. It does appear that interest in this type of research is increasing with the initial work focusing primarily on topics such as human resources management, new public management, and management control and information systems.[30]

---

Applicability of management theories to developing countries: a...-a0141092760 (accessed October 1, 2005).

[29] de Waal, A. 2007. "Is Performance Management Applicable in Developing Countries?: The Case of a Tanzanian College." *International Journal of Emerging Markets* 2, no. 1, pp. 68–83, 68 (citing Pacek, N., and D. Thorniley. 2004. *Emerging Markets, Lessons for Business Success and the Outlook for Different Markets.* London: The Economist).

[30] Design and implementation of management accounting systems, for example, has been frequently studied by researchers. See, e.g., Anderson, S., and W. Lanen. 1999. "Economic Transition, Strategy and the Evolution of Management Accounting Practices: The Case of India." *Accounting, Organisations and Society* 24, nos. 5–6, pp. 379–412; and Maina Waweru, N., Z. Hoque, and E. Uliana. 2004. "Management Accounting Change in South Africa, Case Studies from Retail Services." *Accounting, Auditing and Accountability Journal* 17, no. 5, pp. 675–704.

# Challenges for Managers in Developing Countries

The environment for business activities in developing countries—economic, political, and social conditions—generally varies significantly from the environment confronting managers in developed countries and this imposes significant and unique challenges on managers in developing countries as they attempt to set and execute their operational plans and strategies for their enterprises. For example, managers in developing countries are typically faced with production difficulties, poor infrastructure conditions, market uncertainties and disruptions, unstable and turbulent macroeconomic conditions, financial restrictions, governmental controls, and unstable and under-developed political systems and institutions, inadequate access to reliable information, relatively primitive technology levels, and a lack of skilled and trained human capital. Managers in developing countries must also pay particular attention to the health and development of the natural resources sector in their countries since natural resources continue to play an important role in the economies of many of those countries as they embark on a transition toward greater reliance on jobs and economic activities in the manufacturing and services sectors. In addition, the opportunities and pressures of globalization raise difficult and emotional issues of business ethics and corporate social responsibility. Finally, like managers all around the world, managers in developing countries must understand how elements of societal culture may impact the efficacy of the managerial practices and styles that they attempt to employ.

# Production Capabilities

While a significant percentage of the income and employment in many developing countries still comes from the "traditional" agricultural sector the consensus is that the path to development requires a transition to a continuously increasing level of activity in the manufacturing and services sectors. In order for this transition to occur, however, managers in developing countries must be able to tap into necessary and appropriate production capabilities. Unfortunately, production difficulties often arise in developing countries due to problems with identifying, acquiring, and assimilating necessary and appropriate technologies. In addition, the lower level of education found in many developing countries impedes efforts to train employees how to use technology and manufacturing techniques. Finally, managers and employees in many developing countries have different perceptions of, and attitudes about, quality controls in the production process.

## Infrastructure Conditions

Managers in developing countries are also confronted by a wide array of infrastructure issues. Not surprisingly, many developing countries have been unable to make the necessary investments in fundamental infrastructure areas such as transportation, utilities and energy, and postal and telecommunications. Shortcomings in each of these areas can significantly impede economic development efforts in general and make it difficult for specific firms to operate their facilities, transport their goods and services to domestic markets and depots for export shipments, and maintain contacts with customers, suppliers, and other business partners. However, there is evidence of significant changes in many parts of the world. For example, it has been estimated that from 2001 to 2006 more than 5 percent of the total regional GDP in sub-Saharan African was invested in infrastructure improvements, including significant private sector investments in high-capacity fiber optic cable that have facilitated connectivity of southern and eastern Africa to the global Internet backbone. In addition, the cellular phone market in sub-Saharan Africa has become the fastest growing region in the world with 65 percent of the population within reach of a wireless voice network, up from just 1 percent 10 years ago. Unfortunately, while the improvements in communication and access to information have been impressive, the region has yet to figure out a good strategy for using information technology to modernize and transform other economic sectors.[31]

---

[31] Okonjo-Iweala, N. 2010. "Fulfilling the Promise of Sub-Saharan Africa." In *McKinsey & Company, McKinsey on Africa: A Continent on the Move*, 36–41, 39. New York, NY: McKinsey & Company.

A related infrastructure issue for firms in developing countries has been their inability to rely on local suppliers to provide the necessary inputs for their products on a timely basis and/or at the quality levels that are required in order for the products to be competitive in domestic and international markets. If the government requires firms to use local inputs they must either tolerate the poor quality or invest their own capital and other resources in assisting suppliers with improving the quality of their inputs and the efficiency of the operational processes. If, on the other hand, the government allows firms to import required inputs the managers of those firms must be able to successfully navigate complex rules and regulations pertaining to import licenses that are often found in developing countries. Another issue for local firms engaged in import activities in developing countries is to obtain import financing since foreign firms may be reluctant to provide credit and will generally insist on payment in strong nonlocal currencies that are often in limited supply in developing countries.

## Market Uncertainties

Managers in developing countries often encounter unforeseen disappointments in the projected markets for their finished products as a result of local government action or events outside of their control in the global marketplace. For example, a firm may have been planning on substantial sales to customers engaged in activities in a specific industry that the government had selected for special emphasis as part of the country's national development strategy. If, however, the government decides to change it priorities and devote its attention, resources, and support to other industries the market for the firm's products will quickly erode. Similarly, planned sales to local consumers may be suddenly derailed if the government announces plans to tighten credit as part of its efforts to reduce inflation. Firms in developing countries are also highly vulnerable to shocks in the global economy, such as the widespread and ongoing recessionary conditions in a number of industrial countries that began in 2008 and extended for several years, that can reduce foreign demand for the exports and/or the prices they are able to obtain for such exports in foreign markets.

Decades ago managers in developing countries with a product or service that was new to the local market generally had the advantage of being able to launch their product or service without significant immediate competition. This did not necessarily assure the commercial success of the product or service, since it was still necessary to develop local demand and settle on a price that satisfied local buyers and still generated a reasonable profit; however, managers usually had time to develop and implement their plans and secure the benefits of being the "first mover" in the marketplace. Today, however, the situation is often quite different as globalization of the economy, technological advances, and governmental policies conspire to create intense competition in developing countries, particularly in areas populated by consumers with income earned from jobs in rapidly growing industrialized sectors that have benefited from inbound foreign investment. Developing country managers must now contend with competitive imported products from developed countries and often find that their government has allowed large multinational retailers to set up local manufacturing and distribution operations in return for greater access to markets in developed countries. Finally, the Internet has changed the buying habits of consumers in developing countries who now have access to more information about products, particularly with regard to pricing and performance features, and the ability to buy products from anywhere in the world rather than being strictly reliant on local sources.

Developing countries have been attempting to implement policies that will reduce the risks associated with market uncertainties that have often hampered sustainable growth in those countries. For example, countries in Africa have been working to diversify their bets on economic growth across new, multiple sectors and statistics indicate almost two-thirds of the growth in Africa over the last decade has come not from the traditionally important natural resources sectors but from other sectors such as wholesale and retail, transportation, telecommunications, and manufacturing.[32] Developing countries are also seeking to reduce their

---

[32]  Leke, A., S. Lund, C. Roxburgh, and A. van Wamelen. 2010. "What's Driving Africa's Growth." In *McKinsey on Africa: A Continent on the Move*, 10–19, 11–12. New York, NY: McKinsey & Company.

reliance on trading partners in the advanced industrialized countries by forging economic ties and trade relationships with other developing economic regions ("South-South" exchanges").[33] Domestic markets are also changing in developing countries as large workforces of younger workers migrate to urban areas, a phenomenon that creates business opportunities for firms to participate in projects designed to improve infrastructure conditions in the cities and, hopefully, leads to the creation of a class of "urban consumers" with sufficient spending power to support expansion of activities in the manufacturing and services sectors based on local demand.

## Macroeconomic Environment

Relatively unstable and turbulent macroeconomic environments in development countries also contribute to the challenges confronting managers in those countries in their planning activities. For example, while many developing countries have been doing a relatively good job in recent years in managing inflationary pressures, they are nonetheless vulnerable to high inflation and when this occurs managers of local firms inevitably find themselves battling with changed assumptions about pricing, extending credit terms to their customers, negotiating terms of payment with their suppliers, and obtaining bank financing for both short-term cash needs and long-term investment. Foreign and balance-of-payment issues often impact the business plans of developing country managers. In many instances, governments of developing countries enlist the assistance of private sector firms in closing balance-of-payment gaps by requiring that they increase export activities as a condition to being allowed to continue importing raw materials need for their production processes. Finally, the

---

[33] Id. at p. 13. Okonjo-Iweala estimated that sub-Saharan Africa has almost tripled its level of exports since 1990 and the share of exports to the United States and the EU fell from 73% to 49% during that period while the volume of the region's exports to China experienced a specular rise from just $64 million to over $13 billion. Okonjo-Iweala, N. 2010. "Fulfilling the Promise of Sub-Saharan Africa." In *McKinsey & Company, McKinsey on Africa: A Continent on the Move*, 36–41, 38. New York, NY: McKinsey & Company.

macroeconomic environment confronting developing country managers is susceptible to the mandates of foreign governments and international financial organizations such as the World Bank, which routinely impose conditions on loans and other forms of economic aid to developing countries that have a significant impact on local firms and overall political conditions in those countries.

## Availability of Capital and Credit

Developing countries, by definition, have low income levels and generally suffer from a lack of available capital and credit. The low income levels translate into low demand and this is an issue that local firms must be able to overcome in order to build their businesses. While local firms may be able to improve the quality of their products and the efficiency of the production processes, these advance will be of little help unless they can find ways to attract local customers. Managers in developing countries must act carefully in selecting items for their product lines to ensure that they are consistent with the immediate needs of consumers given their income levels. In addition, managers should focus on creating opportunities to purchase goods on credit, realizing that local financial institutions are likely to be underdeveloped and unable to provide consumer credit tools until the economy has achieved further development. A related issue in developing countries is skewed income distribution, a situation that impacts decisions on which types of products to focus on and how products should be marketed. Managers in developing countries must be particularly mindful of the existence of distinct marketing segments, such as an emerging "middle class" that may have more disposable income to spend on products that would simply not be a realistic purchase for consumers that remain at the lower levels of the income scale.

While the situation is improving and one can now observe relatively developed financial markets in developing regions such as Africa where the situation had been dire for decades,[34] it is still generally true that financial

---

[34] Okonjo-Iweala has noted recent improvements in financial market conditions in Botswana, Cape Verde, Ghana, Kenya, Mauritius, Mozambique, Namibia, Nigeria, Seychelles, South Africa, Tanzania, Uganda, and Zambia.

systems and institutions in developing countries are much weaker than in developed countries. Formal capital markets, including stock exchanges, are primitive or nonexistent in many instances and developing countries lack the knowledge, technology, and trained personnel to establish banking systems that can attract and mobilize savings and this means that wealth is often held in the form on non-monetary assets such as precious gems and livestock. When banking systems do exist they are typically owned and operated by the national government and are thus "heavily bureaucratized and politicized."[35] All of this means that managers in developing countries are more likely to have to fend in a financial system where informal transactions are the norm; fewer financing options are available; and transactions, when they do occur, take longer and are more costly. In order to survive and thrive in such a situation, managers must learn to be innovative in financing their businesses and explore alternative sources such as members of their family and personal networks, suppliers, and customers.

## Political Systems and Institutions

Managers in developing countries typically act, and must make decisions, in a political environment that is much different than what is normally found in developed countries. Political conditions in developing countries are often more turbulent than in industrialized countries, particularly in those developing countries that are struggling to adopt and institutionalize reforms of executive, legislative, and judicial activities. Armed conflict, and often outright civil war, is still commonplace in many parts of the developing world and managers attempting to operate in such an environment must deal with pressures from both the incumbent government and the "opposition." Even when political conditions in a developing country are relatively stable, managers in that country must pay particular

Okonjo-Iweala, N. 2010. "Fulfilling the Promise of Sub-Saharan Africa." In *McKinsey & Company, McKinsey on Africa: A Continent on the Move*, 36–41, 37. New York, NY: McKinsey & Company.

[35] Austin, J. 2002. *Managing in Developing Countries: Strategic Analysis and Operating Techniques*, 48. New York, NY: Free Press.

attention to the goals and strategies that the national government is pursuing in the name of economic growth and development. In comparison to industrialized countries, national governments in development countries can and do exert much more influence on the local business environment and, as such, it is imperative for managers in those countries to gather and analyze information regarding government-led initiatives and to gain access to government officials in a position to assist firms seeking financial support and opportunities to participate in preferred projects. However, the dominant role of the national government in many developing countries has contributed to the relatively high incidence of corruption found in such countries as both local and foreign firms seek access to government officials who can provide favors with respect to allocations of funds and contracts and issuance of required licenses and permits.

Austin noted that differences in the political environment can be tracked on at least four difference dimensions or variables: instability, which is generally inversely related to the level of economic development; ideology, which displays itself in the government's beliefs, policies, and actions with respect to the role of the state and the private sector, the recognition of property rights and the choice of form of political system; institutions, which are generally weak and under-resourced in developing countries; and international linkages, with developing countries being largely dependent while developed countries enjoy greater autonomy.[36] Austin correctly pointed out that economic and political development often does not proceed at the same pace and it is common to see countries progress relatively quickly with respect to economic growth while their political institutions mature much more slowly. In any event, the relatively uncertain political environment in many developing countries has a number of significant consequences for managers in those countries: opportunities for business partnership with foreign firms may be inhibited by their perception of an unacceptable level of political risk; instability raised concerns about shifting national goals and priorities and sudden and unforeseen shifts in allocation of public resources; security concerns; and changes in government may trigger changes in international linkages

---

[36] Austin, J. 2002. *Managing in Developing Countries: Strategic Analysis and Operating Techniques*, 57. New York, NY: Free Press.

that impair available export and import channels for firms in developing countries. In order to survive and thrive, astute managers must develop and maintain relationships with a wide range of political actors and learn how to skillfully negotiate to protect the interests of their firms. Some firms in developing countries are able to insulate themselves from domestic political instability by forging relationships with key foreign investors.

Political instability has been repeatedly cited as a major impediment for attracting foreign investment to developing countries and there are signs that improvements are being made even in areas that have historically been viewed as especially problematic. In Africa, for example, governments have begun to improve their domestic regulatory environments by relying on public ratings such as the World Bank's "Doing Business" surveys as a means for benchmarking their performance against other countries seeking foreign capital and technology.[37] As a result, many countries in Africa implemented economic reforms that significantly eased the path for launching and conducting business activities.[38] Leke et al. praised African countries for making tough decisions to implement an array of internal structural changes such as increasing political stability due to cessation of armed conflicts; and implementing "pro-market" policies such as privatization of state-owned enterprises, liberalizing trade opportunities, lowering corporate taxes, introducing improvements to regulatory and legal systems, and investing in initiatives that improved both physical and social infrastructure conditions.[39]

---

[37] Collier, P. 2010. "The Case for Investing in Africa." In *McKinsey & Company, McKinsey on Africa: A Continent on the Move*, 60–63, 61. New York, NY: McKinsey & Company.

[38] According to Okonjo-Iweala, during 2008–2009 Rwanda completed seven reforms, Mauritius six, and Burkina Faso and Sierra Leone five each, and Rwanda and Liberia were recognized as being among the top reformers in 2010 in rankings constructed by the International Monetary Fund and the World Bank. Okonjo-Iweala, N. 2010. "Fulfilling the Promise of Sub-Saharan Africa." In *McKinsey & Company, McKinsey on Africa: A Continent on the Move*, 36–41, 37. New York, NY: McKinsey & Company.

[39] Leke, A., S. Lund, C. Roxburgh, and A. van Wamelen. 2010. "What's Driving Africa's Growth." In *McKinsey & Company, McKinsey on Africa: A Continent on the Move*, 10–19, 12. New York, NY: McKinsey & Company.

## Access to Reliable Information

Planning by managers in developing countries is hindered by the lack of reliable information on issues that are relevant to the conduct of their businesses. In comparison to industrialized countries, the mechanisms for collecting, cataloging, and disseminating information in developing countries are rudimentary and often nonexistent. Governments do not have the resources and technology to act as a central repository of valuable information on key topics such as supply and demand, pricing, demographic data, availability of technology, and financing, and the content of governmental regulations and developing countries also suffer from a lack of the financial and human capital needed to support alternative sources of information such as trade associations and journals, newspapers, and television/radio outlets. Even in those developing countries where the information systems are relatively mature, many areas of the country, particularly rural areas far from the cities, remain fairly isolated. The consequences of poor information for managers have been succinctly described by Austin: "Imperfect information leads to market inefficiencies and increased transactions costs. Decisions must often be made with a smaller and less reliable data base. Word of mouth information and personal communications networks become more important in companies' management information systems."[40]

## Technological Levels

Very often the technological level in developing countries is low; the technological development that does occur is concentrated, meaning that new technologies are generally not adequately disseminated throughout the country; and there is a heavy dependence on foreign technologies. Lack of financial and human capital explains much of the deficiency in the technological base of developing countries and such countries also lack the infrastructure to launch meaningful technological development activities. Some formerly developing countries, particularly in Asia, have overcome these challenges by implementing government-led initiatives to achieve

---

[40] Austin, J. 2002. *Managing in Developing Countries: Strategic Analysis and Operating Techniques*, 55–56. New York, NY: Free Press.

competitiveness in specific technological areas through public-private sector collaborations. In general, however, the modern technology that is found in developing countries tends to be concentrated in larger companies and specific sectors and many of the firms in those countries seek to survive with rudimentary tools and production processes.

While managers in developing countries can attempt to develop their own technologies, assuming they are able to overcome the lack of other resources mentioned earlier, for the time being it is more likely that the main technological issue for those managers will be identifying appropriate technologies that can be licensed or acquired from other sources and, just as importantly, adapting those technologies to suit the specific requirements of their local environments. Adaptation can take a variety of forms including changes to the technology itself or investing in training and education programs for employees in developing countries that will allow them to effectively deploy the technologies in the operational activities of the firm. The need for adaptation dictates that licensing and similar arrangements much normally include technical assistance from the party that is providing the technology. Acquisition of technology from foreign sources, a process that is often referred to as "technology transfer" has been a consistent source of controversy in relations between the "North" and "South." Many years ago, developing countries often insisted that foreign licensors cede almost all ownership rights in their technologies as a condition of allowing the licensor to conduct business in those countries. As it became clear that licensees from industrialized countries would resist such conditions and withhold new and valuable technologies from licensing arrangements developing countries began to ease their demands with respect to the conditions of technology transfer agreements. Nonetheless, the flow of technology from industrialized to developing countries remains problematic given that industrialized countries remain justifiably concerned about the existence and efficacy of laws and practices to protect intellectual property rights in many developing countries.

## Quality of Human Capital

Many scholars and policymakers have bemoaned the relative deficiencies of human capital, as measured by factors based on education, training, health, nutrition, and housing, in developing countries. The quality of the human capital in a country is said to impact the level of human labor productivity in that country and is enhanced by investing in activities that will increase knowledge within the labor force and their ability to apply that knowledge to production. Interestingly, human capital was long ignored in the standard neoclassical production function; however, it is now generally accepted that investment in human capital can and does make a significant contribution to economic growth. Human capital is a complex issue even in developed countries and improvements in developing countries require not only attention to creating access to basic education for all members of society in developing countries but also providing those old enough to work productively with the training necessary for them to perform the jobs that are available in the economy. Food, health services, and housing must also be available to workers and their families to ensure that workers will be fit and available to report for work without concern for those who look to them for fulfillment of basic needs. Other issues relevant to human capital in developing countries include often controversial policies regarding the number of children each family is allowed to have and policies relating to the migration of workers from rural to urban areas. Moreover, productivity is not only an issue for manufacturing activities and human capital initiatives can but also must include training in technologies that will improve yields in the agricultural sectors that will continue to be significant contributors to growth in developing countries even as they transition toward greater dependence on manufacturing and services.

Managers in developing countries recognize that many of the inputs for the improvement of human capital in their countries must necessarily be provided on a large scale by governments of those countries, often in partnership with international aid organizations. For their part, governments of developing countries have often struggled to find the capital necessary to fund investments in human capital; however, there are signs that changes are occurring. In Africa, for example, governments realize that the large numbers of young people in their countries can serve as the foundation for strong increases in GDP per capita if they can provide education, training, and jobs to younger workers so they can become meaningful contributors to both production and consumption.[41] Also of interest is the increase in private sector initiatives to expand and improve educational opportunities in developing countries.[42] While all of this is encouraging, the reality for many developing country managers is that large portions of their workforce still do not have the basic education and specific technical skills needed to achieve productivity gains at the speed required to assure competitiveness.

Historically, enterprise training in developing countries was limited to larger firms that already employed an educated and skilled workforce, made investments in research and development, implemented quality control methods, and relied on foreign investment.[43] The current challenge is for small- and medium-sized enterprises in developing countries to find ways to implement their own training and development programs; however, many proprietors of such enterprises are understandably concerned that their investments in training will be lost when workers take their newfound skills to other employers offering higher wages. Beudry and Francois commented on the difficulties that employers face in appropriating the anticipated returns on their investment in training their employers and noted that the issue turns on whether the countries in which the employers are operating have appropriate "institutions" in place such as the "labor markets with significant worker bonding" found in Japan and Korea or the "cooperative training system" often associated with Germany.[44] Developing country managers in many countries must

[41] Leke, A., S. Lund, C. Roxburgh, and A. van Wamelen. 2010. "What's Driving Africa's Growth." In *McKinsey & Company, McKinsey on Africa: A Continent on the Move*, 10–19, 14. New York, NY: McKinsey & Company.

[42] See, e.g., Okwu, A., R. Obiakor, O. Oluwalaiye, and T. Obiwuru. 2011. "A Decade of Private Sector Initiative in Tertiary Education in Nigeria: Impact Analysis on Human Capital Development." *European Journal of Social Sciences* 26, no. 4, pp. 598–608.

[43] Tan, H., and G. Batra. September 1996. *Enterprise Training in Developing Countries: Overview of Incidence, Determinants, and Productivity Outcomes.* Washington, DC: The World Bank—Private Sector Development Department.

[44] See Beudry, P., and P. Francois. 2005. "Managerial Skills Acquisition and the Theory of Economic Development." *Review of Economic Studies* 77, no. 1, pp. 90–126.

also contend with the migratory habits of local workers which often cause some of the more promising candidates to move outside of the country in pursuit of what are perceived to be better educational and professional opportunities.

One issue with respect to human capital confronting managers in developing countries is introducing modernized performance appraisal techniques that can be used for decisions regarding compensation and promotion. One commentator observed that while performance-oriented staff appraisal systems have been tried in many developing countries, "[t]hese have not been very successful because ... in many developing countries promotion is still linked to seniority or to relations ... [and] [a]ttempts to use performance targets have produced mixed results."[45] Another researcher focusing on Southeast Asia pointed out that the current practice in most countries in that region "is predominantly old-style performance appraisal in highly centralized, bureaucratic, hierarchical systems with inadequate management expertise."[46] He recommended that public and private enterprises in those countries need to grant more autonomy to the managers responsible for achieving results and allow them to make hiring, firing, promotion, and compensation decisions based on performance appraisal systems that are supported by a regular practice of informing subordinates about the anticipated competencies associated with their positions.

## Role of Natural Resources

The contribution of natural resources to a national economy is a measure of the level of development and, in general, the evidence is clear that low-income developing countries tend to rely heavily on national

---

[45] de Waal, A. 2007. "Is Performance Management Applicable in Developing Countries?: The Case of a Tanzanian College." *International Journal of Emerging Markets* 2, no. 1, pp. 68–83.

[46] Bandaranayake, D. 2001. *Assessing Performance Management of Human Resources for Health in South-East Asian Countries: Aspects of Quality and Outcome.* Geneva: World Health Organization—Department of Organization of Health Services Delivery.

resources and are often extremely dependent on global demand for a limited line of commodities (e.g., the economic health of oil-producing countries is tied to oil production and sales and Columbia's prospects during the 1970s and 1980s rose or fell on coffee prices). Managers in developing countries are advised to stay focused on activities and developments in the agricultural sector even if their firms are not directly involved in agricultural activities. The performance of the agricultural sector will have a substantial impact on the overall growth of the entire national economy and it is likely that a significant amount of governmental resources will be showered on agricultural activities. A rise in the income-level of participants in the agricultural sector can and should have a positive influence on local demand in other sectors. In addition, managers should be diligent in identifying opportunities in ancillary industries which may be born to provide added value to country's primary commodity export activities. In many cases, governments will provide incentives for entrepreneurs in ancillary industries as a means for diversifying the national economy. Savvy managers in developing countries can actually create their own incentives by bringing ideas to government officials that, if well executed, would further national economic goals.

The quantity and quality of natural resources are also important factors for many developing countries. For example, many developing countries are major sources for key basic and strategic minerals that are widely sought by other countries, particularly the wealthier industrialized countries. Agricultural land, timber, fuels, other energy sources and natural tourist attractions are also abundant in many developing countries, particularly in the larger nations of the developing world; however, progress in development of these resources is often slow or nonexistent for various reasons. One problem that is largely out of the control of these countries is that climatological and topographical conditions do not support productive and cost-effective use of land and other resources: there may be insufficient rainfall for farming or mountainous terrain may make it too expensive to access and develop parts of the country. In other instances, however, the main issue confronting managers in developing countries with respect to building businesses based on natural resources has been obtaining the necessary capital and technology since both of those factors of production are habitually in short supply in developing countries.

While gaining access to capital and technology was often seen as an overwhelming hurdle for companies in developing countries, managers who were competent in identifying and negotiating "politically acceptable" collaborative arrangements with foreign investors, such as joint ventures or technology licenses, have been able to advance quickly and establish important competitive advantages for their firms that became even more valuable as the local economy began to grow.[47] Foreign investment in developing countries has often been a matter of great controversy and debate. Many developing countries initially resisted foreign participation in their economies and when such participation was allowed it was subjected to complex and restrictive regulation including the need for governmental approvals. In many instances, foreign investment would only be politically acceptable if a local partner was involved and the investment took the form of a joint venture that was majority-owned by the local partner. As time has gone by, however, developing countries have eased their restrictions on foreign investment after realizing that they were often counterproductive and inhibited access to badly needed capital, technology, and opportunities to train local workers.

## Business Practices and Ethics and Corporate Social Responsibility

Ethics and corporate social responsibility, including the well-publicized issues surrounding "corruption" and "bribery," are important considerations for managers all around the world; however, added complexity arises in developing countries where different societal values may apply to day-to-day activities and transactions in a business context. For example, the domestic lobbying activities carried out by US companies and industries may be considered unethical in other countries and the US practice of "tipping" for services often puzzles people from different parts of the world who wonder why someone is being given something extra for simply carry out the duties and responsibilities of their jobs. On the other hand, payments to government officials regularly made and expected in

---

[47] Austin, J. 2002. *Managing in Developing Countries: Strategic Analysis and Operating Techniques*, 44. New York, NY: Free Press.

many developing countries, typically to receive some form of preferential treatment, are prohibited in the United States and other industrialized countries and the apparent need for such payments in developing countries is seen as an unsettling indicator of corruption and lack of transparency that frightens prospective foreign investors. There is tremendous external pressure on managers in developing countries to embrace notions of business ethics heralded in the industrialized countries and this will require attention to training personnel throughout the organizational structure of enterprises in developing countries and often overcoming local cultural norms.

A related pressure on managers in developing countries arises from exposure to the more extensive regulatory frameworks in industrialized countries. Puckett observed that "child labor is still common in many parts of the developing world, slavery continues, harmful pesticides are allowed, environmental protection is lax, [and] working conditions are poor."[48] There may be good, or least contextually reasonable, explanations for these circumstances such as the need for families in particularly poor countries to put their children to work in order to maintain even the most basic level of existence; however, as firms in developing countries continue to partner with foreign investors and/or join the supply chains of enterprises in industrialized countries they will need to modify their business practices to meet the standards of corporate responsibility that are achieving growth recognition and acceptance all over the world. Puckett noted that certain practices, such as hunting for endangered species, were not only considered to be morally problematic in industrialized countries but also widely opposed in the developing countries where they are occurring; however, developing countries often lack the policing resources necessary to prevent such activities.

## Cultural Conditions

Culture plays a significant role in managerial styles and practices in every country and managers in developing countries need to understand how

---

[48] Punnett, B. n.d. "Management in Developing Countries." http://cavehill-uwi.academia.edu/BettyJanePunnett/Papers/181413/Managing_in_Developing_Countries

the cultural values of members of their societies will impact the strategies they select with respect to management of their firms. Cultural values influence the ways in which people see their relationships with one another (e.g., low or high power distance) and with larger environment in which they live and work (i.e., time and space orientation). Cultural values vary significantly around the world and it is dangerous for managers to rely on generalizations. Austin has suggested that in countries with the lowest levels of economic development one tends to find more rigid social structures, stronger religious influence, very distinct gender roles, and high diversity with respect to language.[49] Austin also noted that while cultural values do change somewhat as economic development improves the rate of cultural change generally lags behind economic progress. While many suggest that certain cultural values are "better," or more "progressive," than others and urge societies to take steps to bring about cultural change in a certain direction, the more immediate challenge for managers is not necessarily changing the cultural values of their employees but understanding those values and the role that they play in transactions and communications in the workplace.

## Management Processes in Developing Countries

Most of the popular models of managerial activities focus on certain key functions.[50] In the early 2000s, Jones et al. referred to management as "the process of using an organization's resources to achieve specific goals through the functions of planning, organizing, leading and controlling"[51]; however, long before that Henri Fayol pioneered the notion of "functions of management" in his 1916 book "Administration Industrielle et Generale" in which he identified and described five functions of managers—planning, organizing, commanding, coordinating, and controlling—that

---

[49] Austin, J. 2002. *Managing in Developing Countries: Strategic Analysis and Operating Techniques*, 62. New York, NY: Free Press.

[50] For full discussion of managerial functions, roles, activities and skills, see "Management Roles and Activities" prepared and distributed by the Sustainable Entrepreneurship Project (www.seproject.org).

[51] Jones, G., J. George, and C. Hill. 2000. *Contemporary Management*, 2nd ed. New York, NY: Irwin/McGraw-Hill.

he believed were universal and required of all managers as they went about performing their day-to-day activities regardless of whether they were operating in the business environment or overseeing the activities of governmental, military, religious, or philanthropic organizations. In 1937, Gulick and Urwick added two additional items to Fayol's original list: reporting and budgeting.[52] Other management theorists working and writing during the 1950s and 1960s also embraced what has become known as the "process school of management" based on the notion that management should be viewed as a linear process that included an identifiable set of several interdependent functions. For example, Koontz et al. identified the following five activities as "major management functions": planning, organizing, staffing, directing, and controlling.[53]

While the process school of management, and the accompanying similar lists of five to seven managerial functions, has remained a dominant analytical framework, others have criticized this approach. Perhaps the most well-known opposition came from Mintzberg and his suggestion of an alternative descriptive model of the 10 core "roles," or organized sets of behaviors, that could be identified with a managerial position. Mintzberg divided these roles into three groups: interpersonal roles (i.e., figure-head, leader, and liaison offer), informational roles (i.e., monitors, disseminators, spokespeople) and decisional roles (i.e., entrepreneurs, disturbance handlers, resource allocators, and negotiators).[54] Mintzberg's work generated a fair amount of debate regarding the validity of the process school of

---

[52] Description derived from Unit 8 Classical Approach: Luther Gulick and Lyndall Urwick, https://scribd.com/doc/219782116/Public-Administration-Unit-8-Classical-Approach-Luther-Gulick-and-Lyndall-Urwick (accessed December 15, 2018). The model proposed by Gulick and Urwick first appeared in Gulick, L.H., and L.F. Urwick., eds. 1937. *Papers on the Science of Administration.* New York, NY: Institute of Public Administration.

[53] Koontz, H., C. O'Donnell, and H. Weihrich. 1970. *Management,* 7th ed. New York, NY: McGraw-Hill.

[54] See Mintzberg, H. July–August 1975. "The Manager's Job: Folklore and Fact." *Harvard Business Review* 53, no. 4, pp. 49–61. Information regarding Mintzberg's own studies of managerial work was collected in Mintzberg, H. 1973. *The Nature of Managerial Work.* New York, NY: Harper & Row, and further discussion appears in "Management Roles and Activities" prepared and distributed by the Sustainable Entrepreneurship Project (www.seproject.org).

management since it questioned the linearity of managerial activities and suggested that the manager's life is more realistically viewed as a continuously changing set of roles that demanded different skills.

When studying management practices and styles in developing countries a threshold question is whether or not such a model of the management process, which was created by Western researchers working in largely developed and industrialized economies, is applicable and useful for understanding how managers operate in those countries. Punnett cautioned that the model had certain "Western biases" that must be accounted for when it is used for analysis of actions in developing countries. For example, she pointed out that "the process in the model is based on a sequential, logical, rational set of discrete activities" and also "assumes control over the environment so that making plans, designing structures, choosing people for specific jobs, and measuring outcomes are all reasonable activities." While all of this is consistent with a Western view of the world, Punnett argued that non-Western developing countries "do not see the world in the same straight, sequenced pattern" and that the efficacy of the model in those countries may be undermined by different perspectives regarding time orientation and the role of fate and the degree of control that people actually have over their environment.[55] To the extent that there is truth in Punnett's words, which are supported by a good deal of empirical evidence on world views of managers and subordinates in many developing countries, it may well be that Mintzberg's family of roles would be a better reference point for developing country managers looking to identify the skills they might need to carry out the full scope of their jobs.

Models of the management process in various countries must also take into account the impact of societal culture. This is true regardless of whether countries are developed and industrialized or developing. Generalizing about the profile of societal cultures for developing countries is difficult and problematic; however, it is probably fair to say that the cultural characteristics of many developing countries differ from those found

---

[55] Punnett, B. n.d. "Management in Developing Countries." http://cavehill-uwi.academia.edu/BettyJanePunnett/Papers/181413/Managing_in_Developing_Countries

in the United States and other industrialized Western countries and these differences will be reflected in how managers in developed countries approach activities such as planning, leading, and controlling. Punnett observed that "[d]eveloping countries have generally been found to be somewhat more collective than developed countries, somewhat more accepting of power differentials, somewhat more averse to uncertainty, and more fatalistic." She also noted that in developing countries the "need for achievement" was generally lower and gender roles were more firmly delineated, a situation that often led to discrimination against women with respect to property rights (e.g., land ownership and inheritance rights), educational opportunities, and income.[56]

Punnett argued that the collection of societal culture characteristics described earlier tended to push managers in developing countries toward a "Theory X" management style that featured rigid hierarchies; direction from the top down, albeit with modest levels of input from subordinates and a touch of paternalism and parental benevolence; and tight controls and rare challenges to managerial instructions by subordinates. Punnett suggested that the cultural context in developing countries raised serious questions about how managers in those countries should approach the most commonly mentioned managerial functions and activities. For example, she questioned whether planning really necessary if events are predetermined, what good were organizational charts if power and responsibilities are based on personal influence and relationships, and were control systems irrelevant when subordinates are culturally conditioned to unquestionably act upon the instructions of their superiors?

In attempting to explain the foundation for the characteristics of societal culture in developing countries and attitudes in those countries toward various business-related activities, Punnett and others have emphasized the impact of the long periods of colonial occupation by European countries, many of which continue to play a strong role in the political and economic affairs of their former colonies even after independence. Punnett noted that the colonies were in subordinate positions in

---

[56] Punnett, B. n.d. "Management in Developing Countries." http://cavehill-uwi.academia.edu/BettyJanePunnett/Papers/181413/Managing_in_Developing_Countries

relation to their "colonial masters" from Europe and thus were dependent on European officials with respect to a wide array of decisions relating to politics, economic, and business. She suggested that this dependence has survived in the form of a lingering tendency among Africans to look to others for decisions and to unquestionably accept those decisions when they come from persons perceived to have legitimate authority in African culture. Remnants of the "top down" colonial authority structure, with little input from the local level, can also be found in the high power distance and tall organizational hierarchies that remain prevalent in post-independence African businesses. Another interesting observation is that the relative lack of marketing acumen among African businesses can be traced to the fact that colonies were generally exclusive producers for their overlords and thus there was no need to develop skills in business-related functions outside of production.[57]

Many continue to believe that Western models of managerial functions and activities may not be totally applicable to developing countries and the study of managerial processes in developing countries must certainly take into account the unique challenges confronting managers in those countries. However, in spite of those limitations, the next sections discuss managerial processes in developing countries by reference to dimensions familiar to scholars from the West: planning, organizing, staffing, leading, and coordinating. Whether or not these dimensions are "universal" remains a matter for debate.[58] Moreover, even if one can reasonably assume that managers in developing countries must devote some amount of their time and resources to planning, coordinating, and other activities listed earlier, they will necessarily bring a different perspective to due to factors such as societal culture, the level of training of their subordinates, their own prior exposure to managerial training and technology and, finally, the local institutional influences on business activities (i.e., national business systems). For example, Farashahi suggested that managers in developing countries have less sensitivity, or sometimes

---

[57] Id.

[58] See, e.g., Lubatkin, M.H., M. Ndiaye, and R. Vengroff. 1997. "The Nature of Managerial Work in Developing Countries: A Limited Test of the Universalist Hypothesis." *Journal of International Business Studies* 28, no. 4, pp. 711–33.

even no response, to competition and economic objectives given the reality that firms in developing countries remain so dependent on central governments that strictly control the allocation of resources and dictate plans to both public and private sector enterprises.[59] Farashahi also suggested that managers in developing countries are very sensitive to social relations and political objectives, which may impact staffing policies and decisions, and that they are less used to making and implementing decisions.

# Planning

Planning activities include identifying and working out the things that need to be done and the methods for doing them, in other words predetermining a "course of action," to accomplish the goals and objectives that have been established for the firm. Budgeting, including fiscal planning and designing accounting controls, is an important part of the planning function.[60] Punnett noted that the predominance of collectivist cultural values among developing countries makes it more likely that planning will be a group activity and that seeking and achieving a consensus among group members will be an important consideration in creating and implementing organizational plans. However, the desire for consensus must be considered in the context of an acceptance of power differentials, often referred to as "high power distance," and this means that the planning process will likely begin with managers soliciting input from subordinates but will end with making the final decisions. Since aversion to risk and uncertainty is generally higher in developing countries subordinates

---

[59] Farashahi, M. n.d. "Management Systems in Developing Countries." http://sba.muohio.edu/abas/1999/farashme.pdf

[60] Description derived from Koontz, H., C. O'Donnell, and H. Weihrich. 1970. *Management*, 7th ed. New York, NY: McGraw-Hill; and Unit 8 Classical Approach: Luther Gulick and Lyndall Urwick, https://scribd.com/doc/219782116/Public-Administration-Unit-8-Classical-Approach-Luther-Gulick-and-Lyndall-Urwick (accessed December 15, 2018). The model proposed by Gulick and Urwick first appeared in Gulick, L.F., and L.H. Urwick, eds. 1937. *Papers on the Science of Administration*. New York, NY: Institute of Public Administration.

will have a preference for decision making by their superiors since this reduces risk.[61]

Risk aversion is also likely to drive managers to proceed cautiously when making their decisions and support those decisions with detailed initial and contingency plans; however, when risk aversion is accompanied by fatalism, as is the case in certain developing countries, planning may be dismissed as unproductive given that societal values assume that events will occur based on some of external force that cannot be controlled by the members of the society. In fact, taken to the extreme, planning activities may be seen as a dangerous questioning of the will of a higher power and subject organizational leaders urging planning to criticism from their subordinates.[62]

Another potential impediment to certain types of planning is the society's perspective on time, generally referred to as "time orientation," since a large part of planning is time management (i.e., estimating the amount of time required to complete various tasks, identifying critical milestones or date when certain activities must be completed, allocating the time of the various persons involved in activities relating to a particular project, and tracking adherence to a schedule included in the plan). Many developing countries, particularly in Asia, have a relatively long-term time orientation and thus managers and employees in those countries may be less interested than their counterparts in a short-term oriented country such as the United States in slavishly following short-term plans. For example, Ayoun and Moreo found that compared to their short-term oriented American colleagues, Thai managers tended to have a long-term orientation that caused them to place a stronger emphasis on longer term strategic plans, a stronger tendency toward involving others when developing their business strategy, and a stronger reliance on long-term evaluation of strategy; however, the researchers concluded that there

---

[61] Punnett, B. n.d. "Management in Developing Countries." http://cavehill-uwi.academia.edu/BettyJanePunnett/Papers/181413/Managing_in_Developing_Countries
[62] Id.

were no significant difference between US and Thai managers concerning openness to strategic change and commitment to strategic decisions.[63]

# Organizing

Organizing activities include establishment of the formal structure of authority throughout the firm that determines how work subdivisions are arranged, defined, and coordinated to achieve defined goals and objectives. Put another way, when managers "organize" they are focusing on arranging the relationships among work units for accomplishment of the firm's goals and objectives and granting responsibility and authority up and down the organization hierarchy to attain those goals and objectives.[64] Punnett suggests that the combination of high power distance and collectivism generally found in developing countries dictates a hierarchical organizational structure with power residing at the top and work organized and carried out by groups or teams, rather than by individuals. In developing countries where fatalism is strong the model of strong directive leadership from the top of the hierarchy is a good fit since subordinates are likely to accept what happens "from above" without question.[65]

The higher levels of risk aversion and preference for certainty in developing countries would appear to provide fertile ground for the use of

---

[63] Ayoun, B., and P. Moreo. 2009. "Impact of Time Orientation on the Strategic Behavior of Thai and American Hotel Managers." *Journal of Hospitality Marketing and Management* 18, no. 7, pp. 676–91.

[64] Description derived from Koontz, H., C. O'Donnell, and H. Weihrich. 1970. *Management*, 7th ed. New York, NY: McGraw-Hill; and Unit 8 Classical Approach: Luther Gulick and Lyndall Urwick, https://www.scribd.com/doc/219782116/Public-Administration-Unit-8-Classical-Approach-Luther-Gulick-and-Lyndall-Urwick (accessed December 15, 2018). The model proposed by Gulick and Urwick first appeared in Gulick, L., and L. Urwick, eds. 1937. *Papers on the Science of Administration.* New York, NY: Institute of Public Administration.

[65] Punnett, B. n.d. "Management in Developing Countries." http://cavehill-uwi.academia.edu/BettyJanePunnett/Papers/181413/Managing_in_Developing_Countries

organizational charts and formal rules, policies, and procedures that reinforce the allocation of power within the hierarchical structure and provide those at the lower levels of the hierarchy with a clear and unambiguous of what is expected of them. However, the practicality of these measures might well be questioned in an environment in which personal influence and relationships, rather than formal titles, plays such an important role in making decisions, issuing directions, and allocating responsibilities. Similarly, when subordinates are culturally conditioned to receive instructions from their superiors and unquestioningly act upon those instructions the efficacy of implementing formal control systems to achieve results may also be challenged.[66]

## Staffing

Staffing activities involve the entire personnel function of recruiting, selecting, and training the people needed for positions in the organizational structure and maintaining favorable work conditions.[67] As noted in the discussion of organizing earlier, the preference for collectivism in developing countries means that groups and teams will be important and thus managers making staffing decisions will give particular weight to selecting and placing candidates based on their ability and willingness to work well with others. In many developing countries this leads to a strong reliance on specifically recruiting people with similar backgrounds, including family members, in a way that runs afoul of practices in the United States and other industrialized countries that emphasize diversity. In fact, "nepotism," frowned upon in developed countries, is a common and accepted practice in many developing countries and one also sees a preference for persons with similar ethnic and/or religious characteristics.

---

[66] Id.

[67] Description derived from Koontz, H., C. O'Donnell, and H. Weihrich. 1970. *Management*, 7th ed. New York, NY: McGraw-Hill; and Unit 8 Classical Approach: Luther Gulick and Lyndall Urwick, https://scribd.com/doc/219782116/Public-Administration-Unit-8-Classical-Approach-Luther-Gulick-and-Lyndall-Urwick (accessed December 15, 2018). The model proposed by Gulick and Urwick first appeared in Gulick, L.H., and L. Urwick., eds. 1937. *Papers on the Science of Administration*. New York, NY: Institute of Public Administration.

Consistent with the higher power distance found in developing countries the decisions of top managers regarding staffing are generally not challenged and managers will be expected to make decisions that reinforce their power and authority.[68] Staffing practices in developing countries are also closely linked to issues surrounding age and gender, and many developing countries retain traditional values that afford great respect to age, seniority, and experience that comes into play when decisions are made regarding promotions and compensation. In addition, many developing countries are male-dominated, thus making it difficult for women to advance to positions of responsibility and/or acquire the education and training necessary to further their careers.

# Leading

Leading, or directing, is a continuous task that requires making decisions and embodying them in specific and general orders and instructions, and also serving as the leader of the firm, business unit, or work group and creating an atmosphere that will assist and motivate people to achieve desired end results.[69] In a cultural environment that is collectivist, risk averse, and high power distance, it can be expected that the predominant and expected leadership style will be, as described by Punnett, "paternal or benevolent autocracy." Subordinates in developing countries with the aforementioned social culture profile prefer this style of leadership as providing security and generally place a substantial amount of trust in decisions made by their leaders. However, in developing countries where collectivism is particularly strong the ability of leaders to actively motivate

---

[68] Punnett, B. n.d. "Management in Developing Countries." http://cavehill-uwi.academia.edu/BettyJanePunnett/Papers/181413/Managing_in_Developing_Countries

[69] Description derived from Koontz, H., C. O'Donnell, and H. Weihrich. 1970. *Management*, 7th ed. New York, NY: McGraw-Hill; and Unit 8 Classical Approach: Luther Gulick and Lyndall Urwick, https://scribd.com/doc/219782116/Public-Administration-Unit-8-Classical-Approach-Luther-Gulick-and-Lyndall-Urwick (accessed December 15, 2018). The model proposed by Gulick and Urwick first appeared in Urwick, L.F., and L.H. Gulick. 1937. *Papers on the Science of Administration*. New York, NY: Institute of Public Administration.

subordinates may be less important given that subordinates are already conditioned to work hard for the group and group members will support and monitor one another without the need for large amounts of managerial intervention.[70]

# Coordinating

Coordinating is the all-important duty of inter-relating the various parts of the work that is performed throughout the firm and includes establishing and administering systems for controlling, measuring, and evaluating performance of work activities against the planned goals and objectives. In order for coordination to be effective managers must be sure that they are kept informed about what is going through a reporting system that includes reports, records, research, and inspections.[71] Controls are also an important element of the coordination function and Punnett observed that because developing countries tend to be more collectivist one is likely to find that "goals will be set for groups and teams, output will be measured at the group level [and] quality will be a group responsibility." In addition, because developing countries generally have high power differentials, controls, rewards, and punishments will be set at the top of the organizational hierarchy and reinforced by rules, policies, and procedures from senior management. Subordinates will rarely challenge the controls that are imposed in this manner and, in fact, will often welcome them as providing security and clear direction.[72]

---

[70] Punnett, B. n.d. "Management in Developing Countries." http://cavehill-uwi.academia.edu/BettyJanePunnett/Papers/181413/Managing_in_Developing_Countries

[71] Description derived from Koontz, H., C. O'Donnell, and H. Weihrich. 1970. *Management*, 7th ed. New York, NY: McGraw-Hill; and Unit 8 Classical Approach: Luther Gulick and Lyndall Urwick, https://scribd.com/doc/219782116/Public-Administration-Unit-8-Classical-Approach-Luther-Gulick-and-Lyndall-Urwick (accessed December 15, 2018). The model proposed by Gulick and Urwick first appeared in Gulick, L.H., and L.H. Urwick., eds. 1937. *Papers on the Science of Administration*. New York, NY: Institute of Public Administration.

[72] Punnett, B. n.d. "Management in Developing Countries." http://cavehill-uwi.academia.edu/BettyJanePunnett/Papers/181413/Managing_in_Developing_Countries

It should be noted, however, that while managers in developing countries are generally expected to implement and enforce controls as a legitimate exercise of their power and authority the impact and efficacy of formal controls may be less than anticipated in certain situations. For example, in many instances those in authority in developing countries will be allowed to make exceptions to rules, policies, and procedures. While subordinates in countries where fatalism will accept such exceptions as "actions from above" a continuous practice of ignoring controls, particularly when exceptions appear to favor those with special personal relationships to owners and senior managers, will ultimately undermine their effectiveness. The need for formal controls may also be challenged in contexts where subordinates accept and execute instructions from their superiors without question and/or peer pressure from direct work colleagues imposes sufficient discipline within the groups and teams that are so important in developing countries where collectivism dominates.[73]

There is a dearth of scientific and professional literature regarding the implementation and effectiveness of performance management techniques in developing countries; however, there appears to be growing interest in the topic.[74] Research in Egypt indicates that performance management has yet to attract significant support and that Egyptian firms tend to rely on traditional financial measures such as return on investment and return on assets; however, firms in the manufacturing sector are experimenting with combining financial and nonfinancial measures of performance.[75] Other developing countries, such as Zimbabwe, are being exposed to sophisticated performance management systems through the many transnational companies that have set up business in those countries.[76] In countries such as Kenya, performance management

---

[73] Id.

[74] de Waal, A. 2007. "Is Performance Management Applicable in Developing Countries?: The Case of a Tanzanian College." *International Journal of Emerging Markets* 2, no. 1, pp. 68–83.

[75] Id. (citing Abdel Aziz, A., R. Dixon, and M. Ragheb. September 2005. "The Contemporary Performance Measurement Techniques in Egypt: A Contingency Approach." Paper presented during the EDHEC Conference, Nice).

[76] Id. (citing Nhemachena, W. 2004. "Current State and Future Developments of Performance Management in Zimbabwe." Paper, Maastricht School of Management).

is seen as increasingly important as local firms strive to qualify for ISO certification.[77] Finally, while firms in Ethiopia have yet to wholeheartedly embrace suites of performance management techniques, managers are taking simple, preliminary steps such as scheduling and holding regular formal and information performance review meetings, using new technologies to communicate results throughout the organization and expanding performance management training.[78] A major question yet to be answered, however, is the extent to which the sophisticated performance management systems have been developed for use in the West is suitable, in their present form, to deployment in developing countries.

## Management Training in Developing Countries

Managers in all parts of the world, including developing countries, can be expected to be most effective when they possess certain fundamental skills—technical, human, conceptual, and design—that are necessary and appropriate for their particular managerial level and scope of responsibilities.[79] It is reasonable and useful to think of managerial training in developing countries as having the important objective of building "management capacity" in those countries, both at the national level and within specific enterprises. A useful definition of management capacity has been provided by the European Commission, albeit in a different context: research and policy advice regarding support for the creation and growth of small- and medium-sized enterprises ("SMEs") in the European Union. In a report on "management capacity building" the European Commission noted that "management capacity building has been understood broadly as encompassing all the means through which a

---

[77] Id. (citing Malinga, G. 2004. "Current State and Future Developments of Performance Management in Kenya." Paper, Maastricht School of Management).

[78] Id. (citing Tessema, A. 2005. *Performance Management Tools: Is the Balanced Scorecard Applicable in Public Enterprises in Ethiopia?* [thesis]. Maastricht School of Management).

[79] For further discussion of each category of managerial skills mentioned in the text, as well as how skill requirements may different depending on management level, see "Management Skills" prepared and distributed by the Sustainable Entrepreneurship Project (www.seproject.org).

start-up enterprise or an existing SME gathers and strengthens its knowledge and competencies in four main areas having an impact on a firm's profitability: (1) strategic and management knowledge aspects (including human resource management, accounting, financing, marketing, strategy and organizational issues, such as production and information and technology aspects); (2) understanding the running of the business and of the potential opportunities or threats (including visions for further development of activities, current and prospective marketing aspects); (3) willingness to question and maybe review the established patterns (innovation, organizational aspects); and (4) attitudes toward investing time in management development or other needed competencies."[80] The report also identified three main categories of means that can be used to acquire the needed managerial skills, including training, advice from professionals and/or consultants, and "knowledge sharing" activities, such as networking and Internet research, aimed at finding out applicable information.[81]

---

[80] European Commission, Final Report of the Expert Group on Building Management Capacity.September 2006. Brussels: Directorate-General for Enterprise and Industry of the European Commission, 6.

[81] Id.

# About the Author

**Dr. Alan S. Gutterman** is the founding director of the Sustainable Entrepreneurship Project (www.seproject.org). In addition, Alan's prolific output of practical guidance and tools for legal and financial professionals, managers, entrepreneurs, and investors has made him one of the best-selling individual authors in the global legal publishing marketplace. His cornerstone work, *Business Transactions Solution*, is on online-only product available and featured on Thomson Reuters' Westlaw, the world's largest legal content platform, which includes almost 200 book-length modules covering the entire life cycle of a business. Alan has also authored or edited over 70 books on sustainable entrepreneurship, management, business law and transactions, international law business and technology management for a number of publishers including Thomson Reuters, Kluwer, Aspatore, Oxford, Quorum, ABA Press, Aspen, Sweet & Maxwell, Euromoney, Business Expert Press, Harvard Business Publishing, CCH, and BNA. Alan has over three decades of experience as a partner and senior counsel with internationally recognized law firms counseling small and large business enterprises in the areas of general corporate and securities matters, venture capital, mergers and acquisitions, international law and transactions, strategic business alliances, technology transfers and intellectual property, and has also held senior management positions with several technology-based businesses including service as the chief legal officer of a leading international distributor of IT products headquartered in Silicon Valley and as the chief operating officer of an emerging broadband media company. He has been an adjunct faculty member at several colleges and universities, including Boalt Hall, Golden Gate University, Hastings College of Law, Santa Clara University, and the University of San Francisco, teaching classes on a diverse range of topics including corporate finance, venture capital, corporate law, Japanese business law and law and economic development, He received his AB, MBA, and JD from the University of California at Berkeley, a DBA from Golden Gate University, and a PhD from the University of Cambridge. For more information about Alan and his activities, please contact him directly at alangutterman@gmail.com, follow him on LinkedIn (https://www.linkedin.com/in/alangutterman/) and visit his website at alangutterman.com, which includes an extensive collection of links to his books and other publications and resource materials for students and practitioners of sustainable entrepreneurship.

# Index

administrative skills, 58–59
American Assembly of Collegiate
        Schools of Business, 42
analytical intelligence, 57
Association of MBAs, 128
Association to Advance Collegiate
        Schools of Business, 128

Bloom, N., 9–10, 47–50, 78
Bloom and Van Reenen's management
        process, 9–10
budgeting as management function, 6

Caldas, M., 122–125
Cameron, K., 42, 45–50, 61–62,
        64–67
Cameron and Whetten's skills of
        effective managers, 45–50
cellular organization, 54–55
checking, EMS, 106
cognitive skills, 59
commanding as managerial function,
        34–35
communication among committees,
        117
communication skills, 59
compliance risk, 115
conceptual skills, 44
contingency theory, 52–53
controlling as management function,
        3
controlling as managerial function,
        36–38
coordinating
    activities, 4
    as management function, 6, 36
    management processes in
        developing countries,
        160–162
creating and maintaining trust, 5
creative intelligence, 57
customer relationship management
        system (CRM), 89

design skills, 45
developing countries
    applicability of western
        management theories to,
        120–129
    challenges for managers in, 133
        availability of capital and credit,
        138–139
        infrastructure conditions,
        134–135
        macroeconomic environment in,
        137–138
        market uncertainties, 135–137
        political systems and institutions,
        139–141
        production capabilities,
        133–134
    cultural conditions, 149–150
    emergence of new global
        competitors from, 129–130
    ethics and corporate social
        responsibility, 148–149
    issues in, 121–122
    management processes in, 150–155
        coordinating, 160–162
        leading, 159–160
        organizing, 157–158
        planning, 155–157
        staffing, 158–159
    management training in, 162–163
    overview of, 119–120
    planning by managers
        access to reliable information,
        142
    quality of human capital, 143–146
    role of natural resources, 146–148
    technological level in, 142–143
    as testing grounds for new
        management theories,
        131–132
    value of management study in, 132
dimensions of management styles,
        75–79

directing as management function,
    3, 6
divisional structure, 53
documentation, QMS, 96

EH&S management systems. *See*
    environmental, health and
    safety management systems
EMS. *See* environmental management
    system
encouraging continuous learning, 4
enterprise risk management, 113–117
    infrastructure, 116
    risk identification and assessment
        program, 116
    types of risk exposures, 115
environmental, health and safety
    (EH&S) management systems
    elements for, 111–113
    ISO 45001 and, 109–113
environmental management system
    (EMS)
    best practices for implementation
        of, 106–109
    checking, 106
    elements of, 101–102
    implementation and operation,
        104–105
    ISO 14001 and, 100–101
    planning, 103–104
    policy, 103
environmental policy, 103
ethics and corporate social
    responsibility, 148–149
executive-level management, 55

facilitating decision-making processes,
    4
Farashahi, M., 125–129
Fayol, Henri, 2, 5–6, 11, 27, 35, 36,
    39, 150
Fayol's primary functions of
    management, 5–6
financial risk, 115
first-line managers, 21–22
folklore and facts about managerial
    roles and activities, 12–13
front-line managers, 55

functional managers
    *versus* general managers, 18
    responsibilities of, 18–19
functional structure, 53

general managers
    functional managers *versus,* 18
    responsibilities of, 19–20

Hafsi, T., 125–129
Harris' multi-factor analysis, 50–57
hazard risk, 115
human capital, quality of, 143–146
human skills, 44

implementation and operation, EMS,
    104–105
incentives management, 49–50
informational roles, 15–16
infrastructure conditions, 134–135
International Monetary Fund, 125
International Organization for
    Standardization (ISO), 90
interpersonal roles, 13–15
interpersonal skills, 59
ISO 9001 and QMS, 97–100
ISO 14001 and EMS, 100–101
ISO 45001 and environmental,
    health and safety (EH&S)
    management systems,
    109–113
ISO standards for management
    system, 90–92

Katz, R., 42–43
Khandwalla, P., 74, 88
    categories of management styles,
        79–80
    defined management style, 72
Koontz, H., 3, 31, 43, 45, 151

Lau, A., 43
leadership skills, 59
leading, management processes
    in developing countries,
    159–160
levels of management, 20–21

Mackenzie, R., 6–9
Mackenzie's 3-D model of
    management process, 6–9
macroeconomic environment,
    137–138
management
    Fayol's primary functions of, 5–6
    incentives, 49–50
    levels of, 20–21
    monitoring, 48
    science, 52
    targets, 48–49
management competency models,
    58–59
management functions, 3
management process
    Bloom and Van Reenen's, 9–10
    in developing countries
        coordinating, 160–162
        leading, 159–160
        organizing, 157–158
        planning, 155–157
        staffing, 158–159
    Mackenzie's 3-D model of, 6–9
management skills
    Cameron and Whetten's skills of
        effective managers, 45–50
    conceptual skills, 44
    design skills, 45
    Harris' multi-factor analysis, 50–57
    human skills, 44
    Katz's model, 42–43
    management competency models,
        58–59
    managerial intelligence, 57
    technical skills, 43
    training, 59–70
    traits and characteristics for, 41
management styles
    delegating style features, 82
    dimensions of, 75–79
    formal, 74
    key features, 79–80
    Khandwalla defined, 72
    Khandwalla's categories of, 79–80
    national, 87–88
    organic vs. mechanistic, 74
    Quang and Vuong definition of, 72

Reddin's 3-D, 73–74, 80–87
Thornton's "big 3," 80–82
management system
    elements of, 89
    enterprise risk management,
        113–117
    environmental, health and safety
        (EH&S), 109–113
    guidelines for establishing, 92
    ISO standards for, 90–92
    organizational context, 93–94
management training in developing
    countries, 162–163
managerial competencies, 40
managerial intelligence, 57
managerial roles and activities
    commanding, 34–35
    controlling, 36–38
    coordinating, 36
    decisional roles, 16–18
    first-line managers, 21–22
    folklore and facts about, 12–13
    functional versus general managers,
        18
    informational roles, 15–16
    interpersonal roles, 13–15
    key roles and duties, 4–5
    levels of management, 20–21
    management functions, 3
    middle managers, 23–24
    Mintzberg's "Management Roles,"
        10–11
    models of, 2–5
    organizing, 31–34
    planning, 27–31
    primary functions of managers,
        26–27
    responsibilities of functional
        managers, 18–19
    responsibilities of general managers,
        19–20
    top-level/senior managers,
        24–26
managerial tasks, models of, 55–56
managers
    best practices for managers emerge
        from international study,
        47–50

Cameron and Whetten's skills of effective, 45–50
challenges for, in developing countries, 133
characteristics of effective, 45–47
as decision maker, 16–18
first-line, 21–22
middle, 23–24
planning by, 142
primary functions of, 26–27, 150–151
simple assessment tools for, 68–70
tasks and skills of effective, 60–68
top-level/senior, 24–26
using autocrat style, 85–86
using benevolent autocrat style, 86
using bureaucrat style, 85
using compromiser style, 86
using deserter style, 84–85
using developer style, 85
using executive style, 86
using missionary style, 85
manager's planning activities and skills, 30–31
manager's "skill set," 42
managing alignment, 4
managing in developing countries. See developing countries
market uncertainties, 135–137
matrix structure, 54
middle-level managers, 23–24, 55
Mintzberg, H.
    list of self-study questions, 68–70
    "Management Roles," 10–11
modernized performance appraisal techniques, 146
monitoring management, 48

national management styles, 87–88
natural resources, role of, 146–148
network organizations, 54

occupational/technical skills, 59
operational planning, 28–29
operational risk, 115
organizational context, 93–94
organizational effectiveness measurement, 75

organizational performance, 45, 90
organizational structure
    cellular, 54–55
    divisional structure, 53
    functional structure, 53
    matrix structure, 54
    models of managerial tasks, 55–56
    network organizations, 54
    team based, 54
organizing, 33
    as management function, 3, 6, 31–34
    management processes in developing countries, 157–158

Pavett, C., 43
personal adaptability skills, 59
personal motivation skills, 59
planning
    EMS, 103–104
    as management function, 3, 6, 29–31
    management processes in developing countries, 155–157
    operational, 28–29
    strategic, 28
    tactical, 28
political systems and institutions in developing countries, 139–141
practical intelligence, 57
preventive maintenance management (PMM), 89
production capabilities, 133–134
Punnett, B., 130, 152–155, 157, 159–160

quality management system (QMS), 92
    evaluation and improvement for, 97
    ISO 9001 and, 97–100
    leadership for, 94
    operational activities for, 96
    organizational context, 93–94
    planning for development of, 94–95

resources and support for, 95–96
quality of human capital, 143–146
Quang, T., 72–77
    definition of management styles, 72

Reddin, W., 73–74, 82–87
    3-D management styles, 82–87
reporting as management function, 6
reputational risk, 115
risk committee responsibilities, scope
    of, 117
risk governance with strategy,
    alignment of, 117
risk management infrastructure, 117

simple assessment tools for managers,
    68–70
skill(s)
    administrative, 58–59
    analysis, 65–66
    application, 66
    leadership, 59
    learning, 65
    personal adaptability, 59
    personal motivation, 59
    practice, 66
    preassessment, 65
    technical, 43
Social Learning Theory, 64
staffing, 31, 33
    as management function, 3, 6
    management processes in
        developing countries,
        158–159
stakeholders, need of, 116–117
strategic planning, 28

strategic risk, 115
SWOT analysis, 28
systems theory, 52

tactical planning, 28
targets management, 48–49
teaching management skills, 64
team based organizational structure,
    54
team building, 41
technical skills, 43
technological level in developing
    countries, 142–143
Thornton, P.
    "big 3" management styles, 80–82
top-level/senior managers, 24–26
trainable behavioral components, 47
training, management skills, 59–70

Van Reenen, J., 9–10, 47–50, 78
Vuong, N., 72–77
    definition of management styles, 72

Weihrich, H., 21, 29, 33–35, 38, 43,
    45, 78
western management theories
    convergence perspective, 122
    to developing countries, 120–129
    divergence perspective, 121
    situational theory, 122
    universal perspective, 121
Whetten, D., 42, 46–47, 61–62,
    64–67
Wood, T., 122–125
World Bank, 125
World Trade Organization, 126

## OTHER TITLES IN THE HUMAN RESOURCE MANAGEMENT AND ORGANIZATIONAL BEHAVIOR COLLECTION

- *Conflict First Aid: How to Stop Personality Clashes and Disputes from Damaging You or Your Organization* by Nancy Radford
- *How to Manage Your Career: The Power of Mindset in Fostering Success* by Kelly Swingler
- *Deconstructing Management Maxims, Volume I: A Critical Examination of Conventional Business Wisdom* by Kevin Wayne
- *Deconstructing Management Maxims, Volume II: A Critical Examination of Conventional Business Wisdom* by Kevin Wayne
- *The Real Me: Find and Express Your Authentic Self* by Mark Eyre
- *Across the Spectrum: What Color Are You?* by Stephen Elkins-Jarrett
- *The Human Resource Professional's Guide to Change Management: Practical Tools and Techniques to Enact Meaningful and Lasting Organizational Change* by Melanie J. Peacock
- *Tough Calls: How to Move Beyond Indecision and Good Intentions* by Linda D. Henman
- *The 360 Degree CEO: Generating Profits While Leading and Living with Passion and Principles* by Lorraine A. Moore
- *The Concise Coaching Handbook: How to Coach Yourself and Others to Get Business Results* by Elizabeth Dickinson

## Announcing the Business Expert Press Digital Library

*Concise e-books business students need for classroom and research*

This book can also be purchased in an e-book collection by your library as

- a one-time purchase,
- that is owned forever,
- allows for simultaneous readers,
- has no restrictions on printing, and
- can be downloaded as PDFs from within the library community.

Our digital library collections are a great solution to beat the rising cost of textbooks. E-books can be loaded into their course management systems or onto students' e-book readers.
The **Business Expert Press** digital libraries are very affordable, with no obligation to buy in future years. For more information, please visit **www.businessexpertpress.com/librarians**. To set up a trial in the United States, please email **sales@businessexpertpress.com**.

www.ingramcontent.com/pod-product-compliance
Lightning Source LLC
Chambersburg PA
CBHW061311220326
41599CB00026B/4839